AMERICA'S WORST
GOLF COURSES

AMERICA'S WORST GOLF COURSES

A Collection of Courses Not Up to Par

JOHN GARRITY

COLLIER BOOKS
Macmillan Publishing Company
New York

Maxwell Macmillan Canada
Toronto

Maxwell Macmillan International
New York Oxford Singapore Sydney

Collier Books
Macmillan Publishing Company
866 Third Avenue
New York, NY 10022

Maxwell Macmillan Canada, Inc.
1200 Eglinton Avenue East
Suite 200
Don Mills, Ontario M3C 3Nl

Macmillan Publishing Company is part of the Maxwell Communication Group of Companies.

Library of Congress Cataloging-in-Publication Data
Garrity, John.
America's worst golf courses : a collection of courses not up to par / John Garrity.—1st Collier Books ed.
    p.   cm.
ISBN 0-02-043235-6
1. Golf courses—United States—Guidebooks.
I. Title.
GV981.G37   1994
796.352'06'873—dc20   93-22367
CIP

Macmillan books are available at special discounts for bulk purchases for sales promotions, premiums, fund-raising, or educational use. For details, contact:

Special Sales Director
Macmillan Publishing Company
866 Third Avenue
New York, NY 10022

First Collier Books Edition 1994

DESIGN BY DIANE STEVENSON/SNAPHAUS GRAPHICS

10   9   8   7   6   5   4   3   2   1

Printed in the United States of America

For my friend David Henson,
who played his first full round of golf, in 1965,
at the University of Missouri's A. L. Gustin, Jr., Golf Club
—a bad golf course.

And for Felicity Clements of Sydney, Australia,
because a promise is a promise.

ACKNOWLEDGMENTS

"You write this book, you may have a few enemies," one of my sources told me.

The jury is still out on that, but I've made many friends while researching *America's Worst Golf Courses*. I owe a particular debt of gratitude to the many golf architects who were willing, on the condition of anonymity, to nominate each others' work for inclusion here. I must add, though, that some quotations were taken from interviews unrelated to this project, and such quotes in no way constitute anyone's endorsement, or even knowledge, of my efforts.

That aside, I have to thank Rick Wolff, my editor at Macmillan, for the original idea. (If golf architects can plead "the Devil made me do it," so can I.) I also want to thank Bill Amick, an old friend of the Garritys, for his leads and photographs and for his prodigious contribution to "Principles of Bad Golf Course Design." I am indebted, as well, to Ron Fream, who gave me a rainy afternoon in southern California and a better understanding of why grass never grows on the eighth tee at Blue River; to Michael Hurdzan, who provided me an early peek at his book, *The Theory and Practice of Golf Course Design*; and to Tom Fazio, for his willingness to talk on touchy subjects. To the current and former staffers of the American Golf Corporation—particularly Michael Haecock and John DeMatteo—I can only say thanks for your marvelous good humor and your love of golf courses, good and bad alike.

Many personal friends helped me with leg work and reporting, none more so than my old college buddy, Dave Henson. Among my golf media colleagues, I must single out T. R. Reinman, Art Spander, Dan Jenkins, Bob Green, Pat Sullivan, Mark Saltau, Ted Johnson, Bob Labbance, and Sal Johnson, although none is to be blamed for the result. Karen Bednarski, librarian at Golf House, produced a badly needed copy of Alister Mackenzie's *The Golf Course*. The reference librarians at the Kansas City Public Library helped with many arcane queries. *Sports Illustrated* reporter J. B. Morris pursued bad golf courses through various newspaper databases. And thanks, as always, to the fellow identified herein as "a former touring pro" or "the former Missouri amateur champion"—my brother, Tom Garrity.

To Pete Dye: Number 1 position on my list of "Unpretentious and Affable World-Class Golf Architects."

Last of all, I thank my loving wife, Pat, who transcribed tapes and tolerated my side trips for this book. In our twenty years as a couple, Pat and I have played golf together only four times—but never, I assure the reader, on a good golf course.

JOHN GARRITY

INTRODUCTION AND APOLOGY

The apology first. To all the people I lied to while researching this book: I'm sorry. Here's the book, and it isn't titled *America's Slightly Unusual Golf Courses*, *America's Overlooked Golf Courses*, *Blue Highways of Golf*, or whatever name I made up to gain your confidence. It's called *America's Worst Golf Courses*.

I lied to save time. My original speech about how "worst isn't necessarily a derogatory term" and how the book "would be broadly satirical, an antidote to all those coffee table books touting the World's Greatest Golf Courses" took about five minutes to deliver and left me stammering like a schoolboy selling band candy. The narrow-eyed looks I got from pro shop employees quickly convinced me that subterfuge was the better policy.

In my defense, I make three observations:

(1) The selection process was rigorously scientific—that is, I took nominations only from qualified golf course architects, course superintendents, tournament players, golf writers, friends, and strangers on airplanes.

(2) When confronted with doubts about whether a golf course or golf hole was bad enough to be included, I always paused briefly before chuckling and entering it on the list.

(3) I followed the "two-source rule"—i.e., I felt better about a listing if I could find two sources willing to bad-mouth it.

Some truly bad golf courses are not in the book. America still has dozens of small-town, nine-hole, sand-green courses. But there would be no point in filling these pages with courses mowed out of pastures by amiable farmers on tractors. To be included in this book, a golf course had to be "constructed" or otherwise "designed." (Evidence of design would include bunkers, mounds, raised tees, contoured greens, water hazards, railroad ties, etc.) Furthermore, no course was deemed worthy of the list by virtue of abandonment or total neglect; the golf courses in this book are played by golfers like yourself.

One whole category of bad golf has been omitted:

The clubhouse at Riverside Golf Course, Fenton, Missouri, December 1982, showing Meramec River out of its banks. On flood days, carts are restricted to cart paths.
(John Garrity, Copyright 1993)

J O H N   G A R R I T Y

dull golf. A score of informants described courses that were "featureless. . . lacking definition. . .totally unmemorable. . ." These are terrible golf courses, no doubt, but what am I to say about them? Fair or not, the face with the funny mustache draws the most stares.

Ultimately, the criteria for admission was pretty simple: something about the golf course had to amuse me. I like bad golf courses—*really* bad golf courses—for the same reasons I like the great courses, the Merions, the Colonials, the Pebble Beaches, and Augusta Nationals: because something about them sticks to the ribs of memory. It's no accident that the most popular golf story Dan Jenkins ever wrote, "The Glory Game at Goat Hills," was about a bad golf course.

As a point of departure, I'd like to mention the first bad golf hole I ever encountered: the fifth at Hillcrest Country Club in Kansas City, Missouri. That hole, designed by the legendary Donald Ross (of Pinehurst Number 2 fame), was the bane of Hillcrest golfers when I caddied and played there as a youngster. A short par 4 on a wooded plateau, the fifth suffered from a ridge that ran down the center of the fairway from tee to green. Any tee ball with cut spin on it kicked into the tree line on the right or cleared the trees and wound up in the sixth fairway. Any ball landing center to left in the fairway suffered a worse fate, bounding down a rock-hard and rocky slope all the way to the tenth green, from where the fifth green wasn't even visible. The fifth was a round breaker, a double bogey on the hoof; I don't remember Donald Ross ever being called anything but a "blankety-blank S.O.B." by a Hillcrest member.

That was in the late fifties. Fifteen years later, after many travels and a long sabbatical from golf, I returned to Hillcrest as a spectator at one of the first senior professional golf tournaments, a forerunner of today's Senior PGA Tour. Sam Snead was there, Julius Boros, Dow Finsterwald, and many others. When I got to the fifth hole, I was surprised by the changes: an irrigation system had been installed and the once-unyielding fairway was now a lush, green sward. What's more, a rich growth of bluegrass rough on the left now snared any tee balls that wandered off the fairway, leaving a reasonable recovery shot to the green. No longer did balls carom down the hill into rocks and weeds.

I watched several groups play through, and then Doug Ford came to the tee. The former Masters and PGA champ, probably the fastest player in tournament history, teed up, took a rip, and hit a high hook toward the left rough. "Get right!" he yelled. "Get right!" That's when I noticed another change that had been made to number 5—an asphalt cart path running the length of the hole down the left side. Ford's drive lit on the cart path, bounced thirty feet in the air, and plummeted eighty yards down the slope to the old boneyard.

"——!" he said.

The point being, I guess, that a truly bad hole has a certain integrity and is not easily prettied up. Jessica Rabbit put it best when she said, "I'm not bad—I'm just drawn that way."

The golf courses in this gentle volume *are* bad, and in most cases they were drawn that way. But let no one accuse me of character assassination. These courses have earned my respect, if not my greens fees.

—JOHN GARRITY
Kansas City, January 1994

J O H N   G A R R I T Y

PLANTATION GOLF AND COUNTRY CLUB
Gretna, Louisiana

Par 69, 5,662 yards

Nearest industry: Electric power substation,
70 yards off first fairway

For faded grandeur, nothing compares with Plantation. The white-columned clubhouse actually *was* a plantation house once, and there are still signs of a renovation performed by the Works Progress Administration in the 1930s. But now the old house is a bit tumbledown and out of plumb. The pro shop is as dark as the powder room on a British frigate. Peeling paint and dirty windows present a picture of decline and desuetude straight out of a James Lee Burke crime novel.

And that's the good news.

"I guess this is the worst golf course we've ever seen," says Mike Haecock of American Golf Corporation (AGC), which operated Plantation on a lease basis for five years. "You couldn't get more than three or four dollars for greens fees because the course was so poorly designed. It's just a horrible little track."

The operative word is "little." Plantation crams eighteen golf holes into 61 acres of land, and on some holes golfers press themselves against protective fencing until they have to hit. "It's definitely a hardhat course," says a New Orleans-area pro.

"Dangerous doesn't begin to describe it," adds a visitor from the North. "The sixteenth tee is between the fourteenth, fifteenth, and seventeenth greens—you've got three greens and a tee in a space you couldn't park a motor home on." Little wonder that a local rule reads: "Ball lying on wrong green must be dropped within two club lengths from that green, no nearer the hole. No penalty." Another rule warns: "Never look back—Look forward, Don't worry about the group behind you, Stay with the group in front of you."

Plantation offers other inducements, besides intimacy. You've seen those enthralling pictures of golfers on the seventh tee at Pebble Beach, the wind whipping their pants legs? On the first tee at Plantation, pants legs flutter every time a big truck whips by on the Behrman Highway. "Kids driving by don't have to yell 'Fore!' " says one recent player. "They toss you a note wrapped around a rock." The first hole is also noteworthy for its unblemished view of an electric power substation, just across the road. "Everybody gets a charge out of that," quips a golfer about to tee off.

The par-5 second hole teases *all* the senses: brown water and a suspicious-looking white foam gurgle in an open storm drain behind the tee, while a gauntlet of high-voltage transmission lines defines the fairway down the right side. There are no cart paths, and after a heavy rain it is normal to see fairways churned into muck and golf carts stalled up to their axles in mire.

As for maintenance—well, Haecock can't suppress a guffaw. "It had basically a home-lawn irrigation system, in terms of pipe size. The superintendent would turn on a little valve at the green, which fed a hose to a little-bitty Rainbird lawn sprinkler, which threw a twenty-five-foot radius. That was the green—whatever the twenty-five-foot radius covered."

J O H N   G A R R I T Y

Transmission lines, Plantation Golf and Country Club, Gretna, Louisiana. (John Garrity, Copyright 1993)

Golfers teeing off behind protective screen at Plantation Golf and Country Club, Gretna, Louisiana. (John Garrity, Copyright 1993)

AMERICA'S WORST GOLF COURSES

One time, the irrigation pump went out and the superintendent called American Golf's regional director, who was in charge of area expenses. "The regional director called me," Haecock says, "and said, 'Good god, the pump's out, and that place doesn't make any money anyway. What are we gonna do?' I said, 'Don't worry, we'll just get one at Sears.' He said, 'What do you mean, Sears?' I said, 'It's a five-horsepower swimming pool pump.' "

The pump may be weak, but Plantation can always fall back on its 400-horsepower political connections. The land, owned by the Beninate family, is leased for eighty-three years to former New Orleans mayor Moon Landrieu, his son Mark, and their real estate partner, Hayden Wren. "We didn't know anything about New Orleans politics at the time," says Haecock. "We know a lot about it now, and we're not there anymore."

Plantation's seedy reputation owes partly to Scratch's Pub, a bar and pool parlor operating on the second floor of the clubhouse. Although unconnected with the golf course, Scratch's has provided golfers a few hazards in years past: bikers, coke dealers, and the like. "It's got new management now," says an informed source, "but it used to be a rough place. There were shootings and stabbings up there all the time."

Things have quieted down. These days, Plantation operates as a semiprivate club and the remodeled pub attracts a better class of rock-'n'-rollers. The golf is serene—when somebody isn't yelling "Fore!" and causing players on all eighteen holes to fall to the ground with their hands over their heads. "And it's probably the cheapest green fee you'll ever run into," says the golf shop's legendary Henry Thomas, who's been a pro for sixty-two years. "Four dollars weekdays, six dollars weekends and holidays."

Hey, a bargain!

Shoreline Park, in Mt. View, California, is built over a twenty-year-old garbage fill. "It's a no-smoking golf course," says its designer, Robert Trent Jones, Jr. "You flick your cigarette near one of the methane pipes, and you'll have a real explosion shot. And you may come out of the bunker along with your ball."

FURNACE CREEK GOLF COURSE
Death Valley, California

Par 70, 6,031 yards

Course rating: 67.4

Slope: Pretty much uphill in every direction

Previous land use: Seventh Circle of Dante's Inferno

"Here is the chance to play golf in the most uninhabitable place on earth," enthuses a writer for *Golf Course News*. One wonders what other golf destinations the guy is shilling for. Siberian Gulag Golf and Country Club? Black Hole of Calcutta Municipal Golf Course? Jim Jones's Kool-Aid Links of Guyana?

Don't laugh. Several years ago, the Furnace Creek Ranch began hawking golf packages in Europe. For a hefty sum, Germans, Italians, and French get to tour Yosemite, the Grand Canyon, and Death Valley, with unlimited golf at Furnace Creek thrown in to sweeten the deal. What the foreigners don't know, of course, is that summer temperatures in Death Valley top out at around 130 degrees, with overnight lows of 100. "A few of them come out at the crack of dawn, when it's one hundred and five or one hundred and ten," says head-pro Rick Heitzig. "They come off again around ten, when it's one hundred and twenty, saying, 'We'll come back this evening when it starts to cool down.' I tell them, 'It doesn't. It goes *up* ten degrees.' "

Of course, it's not the heat—it's the humidity.

Let's face it, on any list of potential golf course sites, Death Valley—at 214 feet below sea level—has to be near the bottom. Ask any blade of grass. Summer soil temperatures at Furnace Creek reach 200 degrees: good for baking brownies, but not much help to turfgrass. Perversely, winter temperatures in Death Valley dip well below freezing, nudging the Bermuda grass greens and fairways into dormancy. Rainfall? Less than two inches a year.

In these conditions, even sand traps don't survive. The local sand is so high in mineral content that it hardens like concrete when wet; imported sand blows away in the Valley's furious windstorms. Consequently, all the bunkers on this desert course are grass.

Having painted this bleak picture, one has to acknowledge that Furnace Creek is a garden compared

T-shirt, Furnace Creek Golf Club, Death Valley, California. (John Garrity, Copyright 1993)

AMERICA'S WORST GOLF COURSES

to its surroundings. It is, literally, an oasis—a couple of hundred acres of salt cedar trees and date palms sustained by a natural spring feeding from nearby mountains. From January to April, temperatures are moderate and the Bermuda flourishes.

The golf course itself has impressive bloodlines. The first nine was laid out some sixty-five years ago by William P. Bell, the distinguished designer of the Stanford University Golf Club and L.A.'s Bel-Air Country Club. Before that, there was a three-hole course built by a Scotsman named Murray Millar, who thought tourists would enjoy a bit of poached Prestwick before breakfast. The bulk of the ranch property was otherwise given over to alfalfa for the famous 20-Mule-Team wagons of the nearby Harmony Borax Works. Finally, in 1967, Bell's son, William F. Bell, put in another nine holes.

The holes at Furnace Creek tend to be straight and flat, but the Bells introduced some difficulty by leaving large trees in the middle of several fairways. No one complains; you don't cut down trees in Death Valley.

The layout's dominant feature, though, is a dramatic double-colonnade of tamarisk trees that bisects the course and shades the cart paths. In the summer heat, the wise golfer steps from this shadowy tunnel only to play his shot, and then scuttles back to shelter. Canteens and water jugs are also *de rigueur*, says Jerry Sharp, who tends bar at the open-sided nineteenth-hole canteen.

"The one thing you *don't* do is drink beer out there," says Heitzig. "Alcohol dehydrates the body." When a player complains of dizziness, course workers are taught to throw a towel around the victim's head and hustle him off the course. "But nobody's died since I've been here," Heitzig adds.

How long has that been?

"Two years."

Oh, did we mention it? Summer golf at Furnace Creek is half price.

"I don't know what 'worst' means. Every golf hole has got a cup and a flag and you can get a ball in it eventually."
—*Robert Trent Jones, Jr., golf architect*

OUR DIRECTORY OF UNPROMISING
GOLF COURSE NAMES

Applied Research Labs Golf Club, Valencia, California
Ballbusters Golf Club, Gardens, California
Battlefield Golf Club, Port Oglethorpe, Georgia
Boomerang Golf Links, Greeley, Colorado
Broken Woods Country Club, Coral Springs, Florida
Burnt Store Country Club, Punta Gorda, Florida
Cape Fear Country Club, Wilmington, North Carolina
Carefree RV Country Club, Winter Haven, Florida
Combat Center Golf Course, Twenty Nine Palms, California
Follow Me Golf Course, Fort Benning, Georgia
Fresno Airways Golf Course, Fresno, California
General Old Golf Course, Riverside, California
Hardscrabble Country Club, Fort Smith, Arkansas
Harry Greens Golf Club, Prospect, Connecticut
Hog Neck Golf Course, Easton, Maryland
Horse Thief Golf and Country Club, Tehachapi, California
Jeff Davis Country Club, Hazelhurst, Georgia
Kissing Camels Golf Club, Colorado Springs, Colorado
Missing Links Golf Club, Atlanta, Georgia
Mission Hills Little League Golf Course, Sepulveda, California
Muleshoe Country Club, Muleshoe, Texas
Rip Van Winkle Country Club, Palenville, New York
Royal & Not-So-Ancient Golf Club, Modesto, California
Sprain Valley Golf Club, Yonkers, New York
Stonehenge Golf & Country Club, Midlothian, Virginia
Uncle Remus Golf Course, Eatonton, Georgia
Useless Bay Golf & Country Club, Langley, Washington
Weed Golf Course, Weed, California
White Sands Missile Range Golf Course, White Sands, New Mexico

JOHN GARRITY

BLUE RIVER GOLF COURSE
Kansas City, Missouri

Par 66, 4,580 yards
Closest landfill: Three minutes by car
Special features: Thirteen holes on a flood plain

It's not exactly Amen Corner. It's more of an "Oh my god" corner—four holes of majestic badness on a granite pedestal. We're talking, of course, about Blue River's famed numbers 11 to 15, which sit atop a towering bluff in Kansas City's wooded Swope Park. One former touring pro played Blue River as a youngster and rates it "right at the top of your bad golf courses. I used to go there to work kinks *into* my swing."

Built in the 1920s as a beginner's course, Blue River was formerly known as Swope Number 2 to avoid confusion with the more formidable Swope Memorial Golf Course, an A. W. Tillinghast design. In the 1960s, someone in the Parks Department concluded that calling the shorter course "Number 2" was too close to the truth—thus, the name change. Otherwise, the city has maintained a reverential posture, and no hole has been significantly improved since

> **TEN OUTRAGEOUS HAZARDS:**
>
> *(1) The "bounce bunker" at the par-5 thirteenth hole,* **Loch Lloyd Country Club,** *Belton, Missouri. Balls headed straight for the flag can hit the fan-shaped wooden bulkhead and rebound in any direction, as demonstrated by Lee Trevino in the 1991 Southwestern Bell Classic. Said Trevino, "That's the most ridiculous thing I've ever seen on a golf course."*
>
> *(2) The creek meandering through the thirteenth green at the Jack Nicklaus-designed* **Country Club of the South** *in Alpharetta, Georgia. Ever play a wedge from the putting surface?*

*(3) The greenside bunker at the sixteenth hole, **PGA West Stadium Course,** La Quinta, California. As long as a basketball court and some 20 feet deep, this flat-bottomed purgatory wraps around a shelf-like green and can only be reached by stairs, as the greenside wall is much too steep to climb. Former U.S. House Speaker Thomas "Tip" O'Neill couldn't escape from its depths in the 1986 Bob Hope Desert Classic, so he did what any red-blooded American would do—he resorted to the hand mashie.*

*(4) The Stonehenge Hazard at the second hole, **Carmel Valley Ranch Resort,** Carmel, California. The hourglass-shaped green on this short par 4 is completely ringed by hip-high boulders, strung together like a necklace. Approach shots hitting the boulders are a problem, but the real danger is the foozled iron that rolls right up to the rocks, or, worse yet,*

gangster Frank Nash was gunned down in the 1933 Union Station Massacre.

The front nine, on the valley floor, is forgettable. It's the back side that separates the men from the boys; or, rather, the rock climbers from the golfers. The tenth green sits at the base of a towering, wooded bluff, and the only route to the eleventh tee is up a steep switchback trail lined with boulders, tall grass, and venomous snakes. So tiring is the climb that Blue River's regulars—short-winded seniors, mostly—walk directly to the sixteenth tee at the bottom of the bluff. This leads to dangerous and sometimes acrimonious confrontations with golfers playing off the cliff to the fifteenth green.

Those who do climb the bluff encounter a stretch of holes designed in Hades. The annoying eleventh is a short, uphill par 3 from a canted tee to a crowned green the size of a Persian rug. The appalling twelfth (see "America's Worst Eighteen Holes of Golf," page 32) is a short but unassailable par 4 with out-of-bounds right, a guarding tree left, and a canyon to traverse off the tee. The unappetizing thirteenth, coming back, taunts slicers with another OB right and a huge tree directly in front of

J O H N   G A R R I T Y

the green. Finally, the obnoxious four-teenth, a short par 3, punishes any ball hit long or slightly wide with a plunge down closely mowed banks into the trees. Nowhere in the four-hole stretch can a level lie be found, and the prudent golfer will play each hole from tee to green with a putter.

It's a miracle that no one has ever jumped off the cliff at fifteen. This hole, a 280-yard par 4 with a 100-foot sheer vertical drop to the valley floor, is so bad it's good. Kids and short hitters love it because a skulled or toed shot will still carry about as far as a John Daly 3-wood. Long hitters can reach the green with a 2- or 3-iron, making it the rare par 4 that is

between them. "Nobody's been seriously hurt," says assistant pro Al Norris. But nobody's been seriously thrilled, either.

*(5) The sand bunker in the middle of the sixth green at **Riviera Country Club,** Pacific Palisades, California. Playing out of it is no problem, but putting around it is.*

(6) The tree growing out of the third green at **Stone Harbor Golf Club,** *Cape May Court House, New Jersey. "How do you read roots?" asks Tom Doak of* Golf *magazine.*

(7) Gunfire at the fourteenth hole, **Riverside Golf Club,** *Fresno, California. According to* Golf World, *golfers at this public course report occasional fusillades fired by sportsmen along the San Joaquin River. One player was struck in the chest by a .22-caliber slug—but since the bullet just barely broke the skin, he finished his round before reporting the incident. "It does make*

Sign at Blue River Golf Course, Kansas City, Missouri. (John Garrity, Copyright 1993)

*you think twice, though,"
the victim said.*

*(8) The water
bunker on the par 5
seventh hole at
Reynolds Plantation
in Greensboro, Georgia.
This is actually a ledge
that extends three feet
into the lake bordering
the green on the right.
Players can play from
the half-inch of
water—if they don't
mind splashing them-
selves. The hazard was
suggested by former
Masters champion
Fuzzy Zoeller, who
hates shots that just
barely trickle into
water hazards, only to
plunge to the bottom.
(Note: touring pros get
their clothes free.)*

*(9) The cave in the
eighteenth fairway at
**Barton Creek's Fazio
Course,** Austin, Texas.
Hit your second shot on
this uphill par 5 a little
too straight, and you
wind up in a dark bear's
den with no option but a
chip shot back to day-
light. The cave itself is
noteworthy: anthropolo-
gists have discovered wall
drawings dating back to*

The Bounce Bunker at Loch Lloyd's thirteenth green, Belton, Missouri. (Copyright Ron
Whitten)

The "Basement Bunker" at Dunmaglas Golf
Club, Charlevoix, Michigan. (Copyright Ron
Whitten)

sometimes overshot from the tee. And
thrill seekers love it for its hazards: the
descending trail is almost too steep to
negotiate in spikes, and balls sliced off

J O H N   G A R R I T Y

the tee rain without warning on the sixteenth fairway, which can't be seen from the tee.

To add insult to possible injury, the private Hillcrest Country Club adjoins this bizarre melange. Designed by the legendary Donald Ross, its green fairways mock the Blue River golfer who gazes longingly from behind the OB fence on number 13.

Blue River? "Cry Me a River" is more like it.

the Sansabelt Era.

*(10) The "basement bunker" at **Dunmaglas Golf Club**, Charlevoix, Michigan. Think of the possibilities if architects are freed of their obligation to clear a site before construction! Curbs, open manholes, abandoned buildings, fallen billboards . . . "What've I got, 120 to the flag? Hand me my tire iron, please."*

The Tip O'Neill Bunker at Number 16, the Stadium Course at PGA West, La Quinta, California. The golfer in this picture is average height. (Copyright Ron Whitten)

PELHAM PARK GOLF COURSE
The Bronx, New York City, New York
Par 71, 6,405 yards
Special features: Security is bolstered by frequent police visits

T he golf course is blameless.

That needs to be stated at the outset. People hear the stories about Pelham Park—the murders, the muggings, the abandoned cars—and they think, "Must be a real dump." *Au contraire.* Pelham (with its neighbor course, Split Rock, with which it shares a clubhouse) enjoys a wooded setting in a remote parkland area of the Bronx, seemingly protected from the urban jungle by swamp, stream, and expressway. "It's a course that people should see," says agronomist John DeMatteo. "There's really neat architectural work. On some of the greens at Pelham the mounding is unique, just wonderful."

The problem is, no one can look at the mounds at Pelham without wondering what's buried underneath.

"We've picked up thirteen bodies on that golf course in ten years," says Mike Haecock of the American Golf Corporation. "If you need to drop a body in the Bronx, Pelham is about as remote a location as you can find."

Accurate numbers are hard to come by, but anecdotal evidence places Pelham Park in the top rank of violence-tainted golf courses. A maintenance worker cutting new holes early in the morning once witnessed the execution-style slaying of a woman beside a car on the Hutchinson Parkway. Starters have found corpses at dawn, or people tied up naked and gagged in the parking lot. "You'd be driving by after lunch," says DeMatteo, formerly a regional superintendent for AGC, "and you'd see the police truck sitting in the woods. That's how you'd know they'd found another body."

These killings, he hastens to add, happened after hours and had nothing to do with the golf course. "It was just a desolate area."

But no more desolate than Pelham's history. Built in the 1930s as part of a WPA project, Pelham flourished for some years as a less-demanding cousin of the Split Rock course, which was once a regular stop on the Negro Professional Golf Tour. (DeMatteo says, "There's a four or five hole stretch at Split Rock that I would put up against any course in Westchester.") By the seventies, though, urban decay and municipal bankruptcy had reduced both layouts to weedy decrepitude. In the mid-eighties, the *New York Times* visited Pelham and gave readers the impression that New York golf was played on a *Mad Max* landscape populated with *Clockwork Orange*-style predator youths. One golfer complained that one of his tee shots had bounced into a car abandoned on the fairway. Another said that a car left in the parking lot during a round might not be there when a player returned. Still another said he had been robbed of sixty-eight dollars and his credit cards while lining up an approach shot. "Something like that disrupts a golfer's concentration," the victim told the *Times*.

One insider estimates that Pelham may have clocked 35,000 rounds a year in the early eighties—although he won't guess what percentage of those greens fees ever reached city coffers. "You heard stories that the richest person on the golf course was the starter," he says. "If you wanted to get on the golf course, you went over and

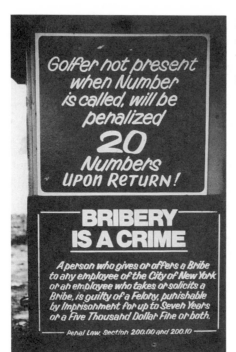

Sign at Pelham-Split Rock Golf Courses, Bronx, New York. (Copyright John DeMatteo)

Fairway condo at Dyker Beach Golf Course, November 1984, Brooklyn, New York. (Copyright John DeMatteo)

J O H N   G A R R I T Y

18

gave him fifty bucks, and you were on. Friends got on for free. Some guys thought it was their private country club, and they were very upset when American Golf came in and changed things."

The changes, made over a couple of years, restored Pelham to a playable standard and shooed away the grafters and hoodlums. Ex-cops and "large firemen" were hired as starters; cashier cages were installed. "There aren't as many fistfights," one approving patron told the *Times*. "It's a country club for the average man."

Unfortunately, the American Golf Corporation hasn't the resources to build a high wall around the golf course. Pelham Park is still no place to get stuck after dark, and that—along with its gory past—keeps this golf course in the top rank of America's Worst.

"It was lovely in the morning, mowing the tall grass and watching the rats hop here and there like bunnies."
—John DeMatteo, agronomist, on his work at the Dyker Beach course in Brooklyn, New York

---

AN INTERVIEW WITH THE GOLF COURSE DOCTOR:

"There's no such thing as too much play," says Mike Haecock, vice president of American Golf Corporation of Santa Monica, California. "There's only too little maintenance."

Haecock is the top maintenance specialist at AGC, which operates more than 150 golf courses in twenty-three states. The firm manages properties from the low to the high end of the quality spectrum, but AGC is most famous for its 1983 salvage job on six municipal courses in New York City, including the infamous Pelham Park Golf Course (see page 16). "We've acquired some truly horrible golf courses, in terms of conditioning," Haecock told us in an interview. "But the courses in New York City were probably the worst."

Q: Is it true that you never saw those courses before you went to work on them?

A: I had not seen them before, nor had I seen anything like them. We took over a course a day, and it took a while for the initial shock to wear off. The first one was at Clearview, which is in Bayside, Queens, right at the base of the bridge there. It's a beautiful track and it does about 95,000 rounds a year now, but my first vision of the place was a smoldering campfire on the first hole, left over from the night before. When we got out on the

J O H N   G A R R I T Y

course, we found burned-out cars everywhere. The flag-sticks were tree limbs, and the flags, where they had them, were plastic trash bags.

Q: *Because the real flags. . .*

A: . . .were stolen immediately, right. Benches had been installed years ago, the concrete kind with wooden slats, but the wood had long since been used as firewood. There were rats in the turf because the mowers hadn't been there for so long. The bunkers on each hole were overgrown up to about six feet with this weedy, prairie type of grass. There was a track through the center of each bunker, and guys would walk through single file and look for the ball. But they never went beyond the path because the undergrowth was just too tall.

None of the greens had any grass, other than weeds. None of the fairways had any grass, other than weeds. And none of the tees had any grass, *including* weeds. It was pretty awesome.

Q: *Was this outside the realm of your experience?*

A: Well, I'm from the private club business in southern California. I didn't realize anything could be that bad and still be called a golf course. At South Shore, down on Staten Island, they were using well water, and the leachate from an adjacent landfill had apparently infil-trated the water table from which the wells drew. The trees were barely surviving, and there was virtually no turf except for a very different-looking strain of what I think was bentgrass. It was almost black and there was

AMERICA'S WORST GOLF COURSES

only one plant every six to eight inches. And that was on the better areas of the golf course—the rest was dirt. I had the water analyzed, and it tested out very similar to the effluent from a chrome-plating establishment. We closed the wells and went on city water, and that enabled us to grow turf on South Shore.

Q: What did you think of the golf courses as golf courses?

A: My perspective is maintenance rather than design, but they were good golf courses. Just in horrible shape. The city was broke at the time, and the courses had to get along with whatever nickels and pennies they could scrape up. To its credit, the city recognized that it shouldn't be in the golf business when it had so many conflicting demands on its funds.

Q: So where did you start?

A: We hired the first twenty-five or thirty bodies that walked in off the street looking for work. We handed them rakes, shovels, and pickaxes and said, "Let's just start working around the clubhouse. Forget the golf course." Because the clubhouse was so overgrown you couldn't find it. After three or four hours, twenty-three of the twenty-five had disappeared, never to be seen again. But we found some local people that liked golf and wanted to work.

Q: When a golf course is that overgrown, can you see its original design?

A: You could see where the golf holes were supposed to be, once we chopped down the growth and started planting and mowing. That's generally true in golf. If they've been constructed at all, not just mowed out of a pasture, you can see where things are supposed to be.

Q: But you found many things where they were not supposed to be.

A: Oh, yes. We found over 100 burned-out cars, maybe 200. Just a little bit of everything, the detritus of a contemporary urban civilization. You name it, and it was there. At Dyker Beach, in Brooklyn, we had a guy living in the underbrush, waiting for his tax refund. He lived in a tent in a marshy area where none of the golfers ever went. We let him continue to live there, since he didn't bother any of the golfers and they didn't bother him. He kept kids off the course at night.

Q: Was that a first?

A: No, we find people living on golf courses. At La Mirada, in suburban Los Angeles, we found a treehouse in an overgrown area totally out of play. Nobody ever went up there, just delivery trucks driving by, and when we went in there to clean up, we found an occupied tree house. That's in suburban L.A., sixteen miles from downtown.

Q: Once you've cleaned up an urban nightmare course, how do you protect it?

A: In those settings, we pick up all the amenities every night. What we can't pick up—say, satellite irrigation controllers—we encage in real strong NEMA boxes, which are further encaged in chain link. Even so, we've had kids get in and light off propane bottles, which causes them to vaporize. It must be pretty spectacular. You can't even find pieces of these boxes, and they're three feet high.

But the real secret is to become part of the neighborhood, to learn to live and let live. At Clearview, we discovered an elaborate bicycle and motocross track over to the side of the eighteenth fairway, off in the rough and well into the tree line. It was probably forty yards wide at its widest. In cleaning up, we took the standard golf operations posture that bicycles don't belong on golf

A typical automobile hazard at Dyker Beach Golf Course, Brooklyn, New York. (Copyright Ted Hardin)

J O H N   G A R R I T Y

courses. So we messed it up, graded out the mounds that the kids had built up by hand.

The very next night, they tore up about eight of our greens. Just destroyed them. So we went back with the tractor the next day and put the track back—regraded the whole thing and made it even better than it was before. And they never messed with us again.

Q: *You had been insensitive to the environment—the urban environment.*

A: Exactly. We had encroached upon something that wasn't really bothering us, and we had messed it up. We learned that you don't just have to cater to the golfers. You have to cater to the neighborhood, too.

Q: *Have you rescued other urban courses?*

A: We took over Atlanta's courses a year or so later, and they were horrible, almost as bad as New York's. At the North Fulton course—Chastain Park is another name for it—somebody had decided to do some irrigation repairs three years before, and they had dug up the quick coupling valves in about four fairways. But that was as far as they ever got. When we got there, three years later, the holes were still there. The dirt piled to the side of the holes had grown over, and they were mowing it.

Q: *At least they were mowing.*

A: Yes, but that golf course had no fairway mower. We asked the guy, "What do you mow fairways with?" And

AMERICA'S WORST GOLF COURSES

he showed us what was basically a very beat-up rough mower. He said, "The fairway mower's been down in the city yard for three years waiting to get repaired." The city of Atlanta is like a lot of other municipalities; they have a city maintenance yard that takes care of all city vehicles. So when you send a golf course fairway mower down there, it gets in line behind the police cars, fire trucks, and ambulances. Atlanta was financially pinched at that time, so they had not mowed the fairways properly for three years. The grass was mowed—or hacked—at two inches.

Q: Your stories are real groaners, but it's obvious that you care about these golf courses.

A: I really do. You play the ball as it lies, and I see a poorly maintained golf course as an opportunity, a chance to turn something into an asset for its owner. When we went into New York in the summer of 1983, the city was losing in the vicinity of four hundred thousand dollars a year on those six courses. We now pay them a positive cash flow on those golf courses, and have since the day we took over.

So yes, I enjoy it immensely. It's a lot of fun.

Q: In every case, though, it seems that the first step in rehabilitating a golf course is to give it a generous top-dressing of cash.

A: Well, it's no accident that grass and money are the same color.

The winner of the Worst Course Award, Olfactory Division, goes to Queen's Harbour Yacht and Country Club, a Mark McCumber course built next to a landfill in Jacksonville, Florida. "It's a beautiful golf course," says Ohio manufacturing executive Ron Calhoun, "but there are two or three holes where you have to hold your nose. You go by this big mound of refuse nicknamed 'Mt. Evershit,' and the smell is atrocious."

The developer says the odor will soon be under control. "It better be," says Calhoun. "They're trying to sell expensive lots all around it."

Another classy stench rises from Bird and Seal Rock, in the ocean off the fifth hole at Spyglass Hill Golf Course, Monterey, California. "Birds have been crapping on that rock for thousands of years," says ABC-TV golf historian Sal Johnson. "On a hot summer day, it's the smelliest hole in the world." According to legend, the owner of the spectacular glass-walled house to the left of the sixth green sold at a loss to escape the odor.

AMERICA'S WORST GOLF COURSES

FT. MEADE CITY MOBILE HOME PARK
GOLF COURSE
Ft. Meade, Florida
9 holes, par 27, 1,051 yards
Unusual local rules: Free drop from ant hills

"I'm going to retire to Florida and play a lot of golf," says the man at the next desk. "Palm trees, high-rise condos, Bermuda-grass greens, golden sunsets"—he leans back in his chair, his hands behind his head—"and maybe a little boat docked on the Intracoastal Waterway. I'll play eighteen holes every morning, and when the shadows get long in the afternoon I'll step out of my fairway condo and hit balls till dark."

Well, that's one view of retirement golf—a view reinforced by the glossy ads in the back of golf and travel magazines. But there are alternatives, and pending retirees should at least consider the no-frills package offered by the Ft. Meade City Mobile Home Park Golf Course. "It's the only golf course I've ever seen that might make you reconsider retirement," says Denny Trease, long-time Kansas City Royals TV play-by-play man. "It is . . . unusual."

Ft. Meade is a town of 6,000 in southern Polk County, midway between Fort Lonesome and Frostproof. The ambiance is Old South: ancient live oak trees draped with moss, a sleepy main street, and lights out at nine. Social life in Ft. Meade revolves around the city mobile home park, which provides pads for 250 units, many with screened porches and other permanent additions. The city also provides—but does not maintain—the golf

JOHN GARRITY

28

course, which occupies a rectangle of land between the mobile homes and the city sanitation works. According to bylaws, the course is for the private use of mobile home residents, and "because of the limited sight range and for personal safety, the course cannot be used as a driving range."

Some might argue that it can't be used as a golf course, either. The Ft. Meade layout consists of eight packed, red-clay sand greens, about 12 feet in diameter, arranged on either side of the flat property like eyelets on a shoe. A ninth hole (see "America's Worst Eighteen Holes of Golf," page 32) runs straight back down the tongue of the shoe, crossing all eight shoelaces (or fairways) to a dead end at the water treatment plant. Holes 5 and 6 cross each other, as do numbers 7 and 8.

"From a land-use standpoint, it looks pretty efficient," a national golf writer concluded after studying the design. "I've always wondered why every hole on a golf course has to have its own fairway."

Short hitters need not fear Ft. Meade. Holes 1 through 8 range from 100 to 122 yards, with only the 142-yard ninth requiring more stick. "Most people play this course with one club," says Trease, "anything from a three-iron to an eight-iron. I play with an eight-iron, and when I get to the ninth I just muscle up."

Trease hastens to add that it isn't the golf that draws him to Ft. Meade. It's his father, Hersch Trease, a former president of the Ft. Meade City Mobile Home Park Golf Association. "You ought to see my dad swing," says Trease. "He's over seventy, but he leaves his feet on every shot."

The elder Trease, who honed his game on conventional courses before he retired, recently switched from an 8- to a 6-iron for his rounds at Ft. Meade. "I have always tried to play the holes here the way I'd play a par 3 on a normal course," he says. "By that I mean, I hit it high in the air. But the older fellows—and I'm no spring chicken—these eighty-year-old guys run the ball onto the greens, and they're tough to beat."

If nothing else, using a less-lofted club has helped Trease on the greens. "You use your one club to putt with," he explains, "because we have a lot of fire ants. Put a club on the ground and it will be overrun by ants."

When they aren't playing or dodging ants, Ft. Meade's members cheerfully throw themselves into maintenance chores: mowing, watering, and pulling moss off the huge oak trees that dot the property. Tournaments, when held at all, are of the scramble variety, undermining efforts by a few to establish handicaps. Says Trease, "It's just a fun course for people who play strictly for the exercise and the fellowship."

Maybe so, but the Ft. Meade Golf Committee met on February 17, 1984, and set down a few rules. Rule 1 states, "Every player must count every stroke taken." Rule 2 reminds the forgetful, "If the ball can not be hit from where it lies and must be moved, it must be counted as a stroke." And Rule 4 is downright accusatory: "Anytime the ball is hit enough to move it, it must be counted as a stroke."

Obviously, retirement provides no refuge from nit-pickers and foul-callers.

J O H N   G A R R I T Y

"If we built some of the classic golf holes today," golf architect Tom Fazio observes, *"they would be considered bad
design. There are holes at the Old Course at St. Andrews
that have blind tee shots and pot bunkers hidden all over
the fairways. By the same token, people like to talk about
that 'great old classic Donald Ross course,' and he's got
blind holes, severe side slopes, all the evils of period design.
People accept it because it's old, but if it was on a new
course, the Tour players would criticize it to no end."*

NUMBER 3, BLUSH HILL COUNTRY CLUB
Waterbury, Vermont
Par 4, 206 yards

"The third hole at Blush Hill is unique in Vermont, northern New England, and perhaps the world," writes Bob Labbance, editor of *Vermont Golf*.

He's not going out on a limb there. The fairway of this peculiar par 4 narrows to a 15-yard opening just 60 yards off the tee, thanks to the subtle placement of a 300-foot radio tower on the left. Local Rule 3 states, "A ball hitting white house, tower, or wires on the fly may be replayed."

Labbance writes, "The magnetic draw of this spire can influence golf balls and the golfing mind of the uninitiated."

Actually, the green can be driven if you're not averse to risk. The fairway bends around the tower, dips into a gully, and then rises to a small green surrounded by lateral water, woods, and out-of-bounds. "The hole itself is pretty simple," says Labbance, "but it's almost mystical when you're standing on the tee. You look at radio towers from a distance, they look big. But when you're standing right below one, it looks *big*."

NUMBER 17, TPC AT SAWGRASS
Ponte Verde, Florida
Par 3, 132 yards

There are other island greens—the seventeenth at PGA West's Stadium Course, the seventh at Stone Harbor, the seventeenth at Red Hawk—but this is *the* island green, the one Pete Dye built to humble the touring pros. During a windy first round at the 1984 Tournament Players Championship, sixty-four balls found the water on number 17, and the average score was 3.79. In 1991, Tour rookie Robert Gamez made an 11 on the hole. These and other horror stories explain why John Mahaffey called it "the easiest par five on the course."

The infamous island-green seventeenth, the TPC at Sawgrass, Ponte Verde, Florida. (Author's collection)

"It's the worst hole of all," says architect Robert Trent Jones, Jr., "because some people can't ever finish the hole. They're unable to get the ball over the water, and they certainly can't walk on it. You've played maybe sixteen good holes, and you can't finish the round."

Some golfers, having completed their first round at the TPC, swear they don't remember playing holes one through sixteen, they were so worried about the seventeenth. The tee shot itself is little more than a pitch shot for most golfers, a half-seven slap for others. But the green looks like a lily pad out there on the water. The panic factor comes into play with the first "splash," because that's when the golfer realizes that he faces the same shot again and again and again, until he gets it right. "That kind of hole at the end of a round is gut-wrenching," says Jones. "You'll have to ask Pete why he wanted to send people to their psychiatrist."

Number 9, Bobby Jones Municipal Golf Course
Atlanta, Georgia
Par 4, 360 yards

Bobby Jones is flat for a couple of holes, and then the golfer comes to a bluff that rises 100 feet. "It was like they didn't know what to do," says golf architect Bill Amick. "So they put the tee at the bottom of the bluff and the green on top." Strong players could fly the mountain with a lofted iron, but low-ball hitters were practically driven to tears. "I don't see how women who don't get much elevation ever finished the hole," says Amick. "They just beat it into the bluff."

"It was one of the ten worst holes in golf, without question," says American Golf's Heacock, who had a new green built to turn the third into a less-steep 165 yards. He hastens to add, "The ninth hole is almost equally bad, though."

Let's just say that the ninth lacks definition. You're up on the bluff, looking at treetops, and the only hint that there's a golf hole is a 75-foot opening and a glimpse of a cart path on the flood plain. "You hit over Tanyard Creek," says free-lance writer Anne Garrity, "which I guess is picturesque—if you can get past the floating garbage and the stench."

America's Worst Golf Courses says: bring back the old third hole. Classic bad design should be preserved.

"I've always held that a golf hole is intrinsically bad," Ron Whitten once wrote, "if it takes a local rule just to finish playing it."

Whitten had in mind the late, unlamented "Jaws" par 3 at Stone Harbor, architect Desmond Muirhead's most-condemned golf hole. The local rule alluded to allowed the golfer a drop on the back of the island green after hitting two balls in the water. An alternate rule permitted the golfer to skip the seventh and play the eighth hole twice while wearing a blindfold. That rule was dropped because *everyone* wanted to play Stone Harbor wearing a blindfold.

According to Muirhead, Jaws was inspired by the story of Jason and the Argonauts, with the boat-shaped green representing Jason's boat and the toothy island bunkers representing the blue rocks thrown down by the gods to crush his boat. From a bulkhead-sided tee, 20 feet in the air, the golfer was asked to land a 6- or 7-iron on the boat's deck. Misses landed in the water or, even worse, in the bunkers, which were separated from the putting surface by narrow moats.

"It was incredible," says agronomist John DeMatteo, who was called in as a consultant when grass wouldn't grow during construction. "I told the superintendent, 'I'd like to have the USGA guys come down here and talk about the rulings on this hole.' I mean, it was almost impossible to hit a shot out of the bunkers and hold the green."

The bunkers weren't just unplayable; they were

JOHN GARRITY

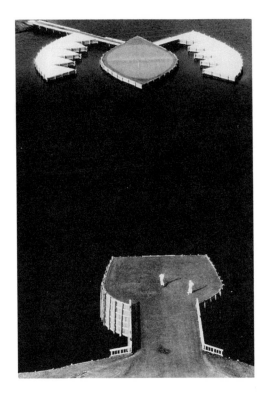

Desmond Muirhead's
"Jaws"—the seventh
at Stone Harbor.
(Copyright Ron Whitten)

unmaintainable. Access to each was limited to foot-
bridges at the far ends, so balls played from the near ends
required the golfer to tramp through twenty-some yards
of sand to get to his ball—and to rake the same on the
way out. Few golfers wanted to waste ten minutes on
raking, so the sand was rarely smooth.

Whitten's conclusion: Jaws "epitomizes all that's bad
in course design."

Apparently, the owners of Stone Harbor agreed,
because Jaws was bulldozed into oblivion in 1991 and a
new number 7 built in its place.

The reader may object: How can a defunct hole be on a list of America's worst golf holes? The answer is that Jaws was, and is, a piece of conceptual art by a conceptual artist, Muirhead. As such, it was more real as a photograph in magazines than as a sand-and-turf golf hole. The bulldozers may have erased the temporal Jaws, but the conceptual Jaws remains untouched—as the accompanying photograph proves.

(Anyone finding the above explanation satisfactory is urged to apply for an internship with Muirhead.)

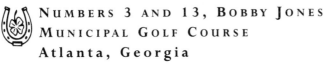
Bobby Jones is flat for two holes, and then the golfer comes to a bluff that rises 100 feet. "It was like they didn't know what to do," says golf architect Bill Amick. "So they put the tee at the bottom of the bluff and the green on top." Strong players could fly the mountain with a lofted iron, but low-ball hitters were practically driven to tears. "I don't see how women who don't get much elevation ever finished the hole," says Amick. "They just beat it into the bluff."

"It was one of the ten worst holes in golf, without question," says American Golf's Heacock, who had a new tee built to turn the third into a less-steep 185 yards. He hastens to add, "The thirteenth hole is almost equally bad, though. You're now at the top of the bluff with Peachtree Creek—which periodically floods out the golf course—running at the base. From there, you drive out *over* one green to the green for which you're shooting. It's still pretty bad."

AWGC deems the alterations to number 3 to be temporary. Anyway you look at it, these are one bad hole(s).

"**I**'d like to dynamite the damn hole," says David Henson, a high-level Washington bureaucrat. "It's darn near impossible, and it'll ruin your round."

The number-one handicap hole at Penderbrook, the twelfth calls for a tee shot of 215 yards from the whites to a landing area about 30 yards in diameter; anything longer rolls into the lake. Drives hit left are out of bounds in the tree line; anything right and short adds to the impossibility of the second shot. The approach, after about a 60-degree turn to the left, is a carry of 180 to 185 yards to a green that rises out of the water.

"You've got a downhill lie," the tormented Henson continues. "Anything to the left of the green is in the water, anything over the green is out of bounds, anything to the right of the green is either in the bunkers, if you're lucky, or out of bounds. It looks farther than one hundred eighty because it's over water and there's no room at the other end. You tend to swing too hard and top the ball into the water. Then the penalty shot is the same damn shot all over again."

Penderbrook's business manager, Larry Beguin, says only that "the hole is designed to be very tough." No joke. A young man at the 1991 USGA Junior Qualifying was even par and leading the tournament when he came to this hole. He took a 12.

J O H N   G A R R I T Y

Par 3, 187 yards

"Worst hole I've ever seen," says a well-known golf course architect. "I think Ben Hogan took a twelve there." Another informant claims Hogan took an 11, and that the great man later called the Country Club of Charleston "the best seventeen-hole golf course in America."

"No, that's a myth," says 1938 Masters and 1939 PGA champion Henry Picard, a former head pro at Country Club of Charleston. "Hogan never even played there. They're probably thinking of 1934, when Vic Ghezzi was leading the tournament going into that hole and made seven there and six on the next hole and wound up not even finishing in the money."

You don't have to go back that far for verifiable victims. Number 11 is the most-watched hole at the annual Azalea Invitation Amateur, providing comic relief for all but the poor souls ruining their rounds with double-digit scores. Both tee and green are elevated above a ravine, and the green is fronted left and right by bunkers 30 feet below the putting surface. To make things worse, the long green runs at a 45-degree angle from the tee and is no more than 20 feet wide at any point. Short shots spin off the green and roll back down the hill, and the left side of the green is so steep as to be virtually unputtable. "It's right by the clubhouse," says the architect, "and the amazing thing is, the members have always been *proud* of it."

AMERICA'S WORST GOLF COURSES

Assistant pro Frank Oliveto confesses that he didn't know what to make of number 11 at first, but he's no longer cowed. "I go right at it," he says. "Of course, that's when I'm playing for fun. In a tournament, I'll lay up and play for bogey. You just want to get away from that hole without making an eight."

Lay up on a par 3? "That's what I always did," says Picard, who averaged 3 on number 11 over five tournaments. "It's a hole that everybody hates, but it's a great golf hole as far as I'm concerned."

Number 14, Wentworth-by-the-Sea
Rye, New Hampshire
Par 4, 415 yards

This par 4 over picturesque Witch Cove calls for a carry of at least 180 yards off the tee, followed by a second shot to a green elevated 30 or 40 feet and tucked behind a double-trunked tree. "That's the easy part," says an embittered source, who has obviously never parred the hole. "The left side of the green is behind more trees, and the green is sloped right-to-left. If the pin is left, it's like miniature golf. You have to bounce it off something."

"It's a ridiculous hole," concedes New England's Bob Labbance. "I mean, I like it, but it's ridiculous. The green is really well-protected, even from the prime landing zone, and it's humped-up and funny to hit into."

NUMBER 12, BLUE RIVER GOLF COURSE
Kansas City, Missouri
Par 4, 234 yards

....

The signature hole at Blue River (see page 11), the twelfth is easily tamed by anyone who can hit a controlled draw with a 1-iron—i.e., a touring pro. Otherwise, there is no landing area. The tee shot, over a deep chasm, is to an elevated green guarded by a towering tree on the left and woods immediately to the right and in back. Fades and slices go out-of-bounds right; straight balls hit the tree or bounce into the woods behind; short drives hit the hill and roll back into the gully. "I've never parred the hole," says a writer who played Blue River in his youth, "but I found dozens of new golf balls looking for my ball in the woods to the right. For me, the hole played 3-wood, snake-iron, wedge, three putts."

Amazingly, the twelfth used to be played as a par 3. "It was one of the toughest par threes in the country," says a Blue River staffer. "Took no prisoners, you might say." The strategy, when it was a par 3, was to rip your tee shot straight into the high branches in the sentry tree, hoping that the ball would ricochet onto the green and not fall back down the ravine. Even if that didn't work, the sound of a ball crashing through the branches was enough to make golfers scatter on the adjoining thirteenth tee.

That's about the only fun this hole has ever afforded.

JOHN GARRITY

....

Number 7, East Course, Pocono Manor Inn
Pocono Manor, Pennsylvania
Par 3, 77 yards

The head pro here says he gets one almost every day—a phone call from some golfer wanting to play "the hole where Art Wall made all those holes in one."

Art Wall, of course, is the former Masters champion, who has shot a world-record forty-seven holes-in-one in his career. Legend has it that twelve of his aces came on this bizarre par 3, which involves a 77-yard tee shot off a 200-foot cliff.

"That's just a rumor," says the club pro, Greg Wall, who happens to be Art's son. "Believe it or not, he's never had a one there."

Those who have played it believe it. The seventh, with water front and left and trees behind and right, is best approached with the image of an elevator shaft in one's mind. "It's straight down," says Greg Wall. "You take it back about hip high with a sand wedge, and if it feels like you're going to chip it into the water, you'll probably be on the green."

First-time players haven't a clue. The locals love it when a newcomer, wary of the water in front, launches a pitching wedge completely over the trees in back. "If it were to be built today," says one famous golf architect, "it would be considered the worst hole you could build."

Greg Wall will argue the point. "It's a beautiful little thing, and there's a story that Arnold Palmer made triple there." But he adds, "I don't know if that's true, either."

AMERICA'S WORST GOLF COURSES

NUMBER 18, CYPRESS POINT CLUB
Monterey, California
Par 4, 346 yards

Our shock pick for America's Worst Eighteen. Even if it isn't that bad, it *seems* that bad compared to the string of holes that precedes it, perhaps the most scenic and challenging in golf. Golf writer Cal Brown, in *The Golf Courses of the Monterey Peninsula*, calls the eighteenth "a strangely cramped and ungainly finishing hole, a shortish par four that doglegs awkwardly uphill past a bewildering picket of cypress trees that give an illusion of occupying the entire fairway. The hole measures just three hundred forty-six yards and, for the good player, would normally require little more than two solid iron shots, but it can be a ghastly experience when the wind is up and the last thing you can afford is an indifferent shot. It is a hole that you sometimes feel you grope toward, rather than play."

It's not so hot as a spectator hole, either. The green is perched just below the clubhouse, but the tee is hidden from view and most observers can't pick up the golfers and their second shots until they hear a thump on the green. And since the tee is backlit by sunlight glancing off the Pacific, spectators are at risk from misguided missiles. The year that Cypress last took part in the AT&T Pro-Am at Pebble Beach, actor Burt Lancaster nailed an unwary spectator square in the chest with a blistering snap hook.

More typically, it's the golfer who suffers. From the tee, it's not clear where the ball should go to set up the approach. Noted architect Tom Fazio says, "You can hit a ball in the fairway and not have a shot at the green. It's an interesting finish to a spectacular, world-class golf course."

NUMBER 14, LAKE COEUR D'ALENE GOLF CLUB
Coeur d'Alene, Idaho
Par 3, yardage varies

If an island green is a bad idea, how about an island green that *moves*? This cute little hole, conceived by developer Duane Hagadone and designed, somewhat reluctantly, by architect Scott Miller, floats on a 7,500-ton barge on beautiful Lake Coeur d'Alene. An underwater cable and a couple of winches allow for distance variation, and a digital meter at the tee gives golfers the current reading (in yards, not fathoms). Access to the green is by ferryboat, and the ferryboat captain snaps your picture and makes sure a print is waiting for you at the nineteenth hole.

When first proposed, Tom Doak of *Golf* magazine spoke for golf purists when he said, "Let's hope this baby dies in drydock." Alas, the fourteenth is amply buoyant, thanks to a honeycombed concrete hull filled with foam and Styrofoam. On the other hand, the concern that putts would roll from port to starboard in bad weather proved groundless—no pun intended. "Aircraft carriers should be so steady," says golf course analyst Ron Whitten.

Another plus: the on-board trees and flower beds keep some long shots from rolling into the lake.

Even so, a basic principle of golf course design is that holes must stay where you put them. Someone should run back to the clubhouse and tell the attendant that this hole belongs in Davey Jones's locker.

J O H N   G A R R I T Y

Lake Coeur d'Alene's drifting Par 3. (Copyright Ron Whitten)

NUMBER 5, HANNASTOWN GOLF CLUB
Greensburg, Pennsylvania
Par 4, 400 yards

Y̲ou and your golf buddies might find this hole to be a modest, unassuming par 4, but Dr. Donald Rinchose considered it the Golf Hole from Hell. The good doctor used to live off to the right of the fifth tee, just across the road. He sued the club several years ago, claiming that duffers had sliced 210 golf balls onto his castle and grounds in a single year. Two thousand dollars worth of trees, planted as a perimeter defense, were useless against the onslaught. The hole needed to be redesigned, the doctor argued.

He argued to naught. A judge noted that the golf course was a half century older than the house; what's more, the doctor knew the golf course was there when he bought the house, making it a foreseeable nuisance. Verdict: no relief.

Whence the doctor?

"He moved," says Ray Bronzie, Hannastown Golf Club's night custodian.

Any complaints from the new neighbor?

"None so far."

Does Bronzie think the doctor exaggerated the problem?

"Maybe. Maybe not. I put a few over that fence myself."

Hannastown golfers, emboldened by the ruling, now aim at the house and play for a draw.

J O H N   G A R R I T Y

NUMBERS 10 AND/OR 11, WILLISTON GOLF CLUB
Williston, Vermont
Par 4, 335 yards; Par 3, 170 yards

Either of these holes would be unremarkable, if they didn't cross each other. The tenth hole is a sharp dogleg left that curls around and passes directly in front of the eleventh tee.

"Williston is a really lovely golf course with beautiful turf and beautiful flowers," says Labbance, "but it is just jammed into this little space. If you're a long hitter, there's no point in taking a wooden club with you. You can do it all with irons."

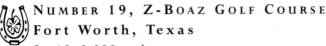

NUMBER 19, Z-BOAZ GOLF COURSE
Fort Worth, Texas
Par 12, 2,000 yards

"A strong finishing hole"—that's how golfers describe this formidable par 12, which stretches from the northeast corner of the Z-Boaz property to the "Checks Cashed" sign in the southeast corner. Every summer, a dozen or so finishers in the Dan Jenkins Partnership & Goat Hills Glory Game Reprise tee off from the blue markers on number 7 and play to the sixteenth green. The journey recreates the sort of cross-country golf immortalized in Jenkins's story, "The Glory Game at Goat Hills." It takes in numerous trees, creeks, and ponds, with a side trip (for slicers) to the Bekins Moving Company warehouse on the west side of the property, just across the railroad tracks. The question of whether to "go for it" or lay up is posed repeatedly, as is the question: "Is this really necessary?"

"Everybody goes a different way," says Jenkins, refusing to be drawn into a debate over the relative merits of the eastern and western overland routes. His own best score? "I did a twelve once. The guy that won made a ten."

J O H N   G A R R I T Y

NUMBER 10, JACK NICKLAUS PRIVATE COURSE AT PGA WEST
La Quinta, California

Par 4, 385 yards

The holes at PGA West all have names, and this hole is called "Confusion."

"And that was exactly the state of mind of the architect when he built it," fumes *San Diego Union-Tribune* golf writer T. R. Reinman.

The architect, of course, is Jack Nicklaus himself, who designed the Private Course during his Pete-Dye-is-a-softy period. The tenth is a straightaway par 4 around a huge, key-shaped bunker that splits the fairway into two routes. Long hitters can drive across the fat part of the bunker, a carry of at least 210 yards, to set up an easier approach shot from the right fairway. Shorter hitters play safe by staying left. What's the problem? The bunker itself—it's 15 feet deep with walls as steep as the Matterhorn.

"You can hit a career drive and miss by a foot," says Reinman, who apparently did exactly that, "and you're down in this damn bottomless bunker. You can't see out, and if your ball rolls against the wall you can't hit out, either. I tipped the top of the wall with a perfect wedge shot and was left with one hundred twenty yards to the green. I'd hit two shots as well as I can hit them, and I was on my way to a big score."

A better name for this hole might be "Rage."

Is there a more beautiful bad hole in all of golf? "I wouldn't know," says *San Francisco Examiner* columnist Art Spander. "I was too busy throwing clubs to appreciate the scenery." Other golf scribes are quick to add their own opprobrium: "Goofy golf," says *Examiner* golf writer Mark Saltau. "The worst hole I've ever played," says Ted Johnson, sports editor of the *Valley Times*.

But it is gorgeous. The twelfth at Carmel Valley Ranch is not in a valley at all, but near the top of a mountain ridge. The tee shot calls for a drive over a ravine to a bi-level fairway lined with moss-draped oaks. The high side, on the right, is supported by a wooden bulkhead running up the middle of the fairway. Balls hitting this wall ricochet left into trees and hotel suites or, if the player is lucky, into a hot tub.

Anywhere off the course is preferable to playing on, because the twelfth fairway runs off a cliff. Architect Pete Dye must have considered this a potential safety hazard, because he barricaded the cliff with more live oaks. Consequently, the green—which is about 70 feet below the cliff edge—can be reached only by hitting over the trees.

"It's an interesting hole," says the Ranch's Director of Understatement, assistant pro Al Norris. "The second shot to that green is probably the most treacherous on the course." This is especially true from the lower fairway, which offers the golfer a totally blind shot. "I con-

JOHN GARRITY

sidered knocking on doors and asking for directions," says one awed sportswriter.

The reward for those who find their way home is a greensite of unparalleled tranquility. Framed by trees and commanding a spectacular view of the valley floor, the twelfth green is an exquisite reminder that quadruple bogies really don't amount to much in the grand scheme of life.

But neither does that *%&@#! Pete Dye.

NUMBER 9, FT. MEADE CITY MOBILE HOME PARK GOLF COURSE
Ft. Meade, Florida
Par 3, 142 yards

The notorious "Gauntlet Hole." From the tee, the ninth at Ft. Meade looks tame enough—a little punch shot with anything from a 2-iron to a 7-iron, if you happen to be carrying one of those clubs. Otherwise, the golfer can slug a short iron and hope to catch a piece of the 12-foot-diameter sand green.

The challenge comes with the walk to the green, because the ninth fairway neatly bisects the previous eight holes. This forces the player to walk directly in front of eight tees, arranged on either side like paddle-wielding fraternity men. "You really have to see it to believe it," says baseball broadcaster Denny Trease. "You aim for the water treatment plant, behind the fence, and then dodge everyone on the way in."

Members say this hole was designed by a Dr. Jack Kevorkian of Michigan.

JOHN GARRITY

"How close can we put the golf course to the airport?"

Developers have pondered this question for years, recognizing that screaming jet engines on takeoff can help mask the chirping of birds that so irritates golfers. Recently, golf architect Don Sechrest presented data to the Federal Aviation Agency that provides some answers. The Sechrest study, which included a "pitching wedge trajectory height map" and a chart illustrating "golf ball trajectory effect on air navigation," concluded that a golf ball can ascend as high as 100 feet. An FAA spokesperson said the agency was unaware of a golf ball ever striking an airplane in flight, but added, "You never know."

A future study will examine the influence of crash-landing aircraft on bentgrass greens.

Steve Brody, author of How to Break 90 Before You Reach It, recalls playing an old golf course in western Pennsylvania, where the third hole was traversed by railroad tracks, 100 yards off the tee. "As I prepared to tee off from the third tee, a freight train appeared round the bend. I hurried my tee shot and hit a low line drive. The train, traveling faster than I had figured, was now roaring across the fairway. My ball found the open door of an empty boxcar marked Atchison, Topeka & Santa Fe, and disappeared. The train was headed west, possibly for Omaha or Denver. That tee shot might have been the longest one of my life."

ALA WAI GOLF COURSE
Honolulu, Hawaii

Par 70, 6,020 yards

Course rating: 67.2; Slope: 116

Previous land use: Malarial swamp

Nearest eyesore: Parks department equipment yard, at golf course gate

Special features: Concert-quality paging system

How do you screw up paradise? Easy. You let everybody in.

Ala Wai is a smooth 7-iron from Waikiki, just across the Ala Wai Canal. It has all the South Sea Island amenities: whispering palms, flowering hedges, late-afternoon rainbows—even a great view of Diamond Head. The trouble is, you can't swing a club without cutting off another golfer's ear. Ala Wai permits fivesomes and sixsomes, and that adds up to 500 or 600 players a day, 200,000 rounds a year. "If they do one hundred twenty thousand rounds in California, they consider that busy," says Ala Wai assistant pro Lloyd Porter. "We're probably twice as busy as any golf course in the U.S."

To speak of the "starter's window" at Ala Wai is to mislead. From a glass-walled command center, former air-traffic controllers keep track of the players and their taxiing golf carts. Meanwhile, golfers wait on a long row of concrete bus benches in the clubhouse colonnade, listening hopefully to the PA announcer's practiced drone: "Kimara, 95. . .Komatsubara, 96. . .Toma, 97. . ." Out on the course, a traffic copter hovers over the 356-yard, par-4 fourth hole, where five fivesomes are backed up (". . .and we've got major congestion on the dogleg at number seven. Looks like someone's fighting a shank, and everyone's slowing down to rubberneck. . .").

The Ala Wai driving range is the best preparation for the course itself; open from 7 A.M. to 11 P.M. every day, the thirty-seven-mat firing line is usually as tightly packed as a Japanese commuter train. By mid-morning, the area 30 to 50 yards off the mats looks as if it's been struck by a yellow and white hailstorm.

Getting a tee time at Ala Wai is relatively straightforward. At 6:30 every morning, the command center takes calls from golfers wanting to play a week later. If you have five or six phones with auto-dialers, you'll probably get a tee time before reservations close, five minutes later. "People say you have to sleep with the starter to get a tee time," says one Ala Wai regular, "but I know guys who haven't."

Ala Wai comes to life early, before the first light of dawn. Singles choke the parking lot in the dark, establishing a rough pecking order for Standby and Back-Nine registration. A sign explains the rules: "Golfers arriving before the course is opened will establish their order by physically standing in line, at the main entrance door, based upon their time of arrival."

Okay, it's not the worst place to stand in line. Gentle trade winds, the sky turning peach behind the dark outline of Diamond Head, palm trees silhouetted against the gathering dawn. . .Besides, nothing says you have to stay after you sign up. "I go home, maybe watch a football game on TV, and come back at 2:30," says one regular. "The typical wait is two or three hours," says another, a Hawaiian. "I've been here at six in the morning, waiting, and finally left at eleven. You just can't get on."

What about play? Slow?

First tee, Ala Wai
Golf Course,
Honolulu, Hawaii.
(John Garrity, Copyright
1993)

"Oh, yeah!" says a Japanese-American businessman from Kaneohe. "Especially when you get the tourists. Five groups waiting, and they sort of putt all the way to the green. And on the par threes, they don't wave you on."

So why put up with it?

The Hawaiian shrugs amiably. "For seventeen dollars, you can't complain."

Actually, you *can* complain, and many Honoluluans have. They gripe that a municipal course should give priority to residents, who can't afford eighty dollars a round for resort golf. The city, trying to balance the tourist/voter equation, responds by permitting sixsomes. The locals

J O H N   G A R R I T Y

write angry letters to the editor, complaining that they *still* can't get tee times. The mayor insists that the registration system is unbiased. The golfers duck errant shots and carry survival rations in their carts.

No doubt about it: Ala Wai is Paradise Lost.

Red-faced officials at the Bayshore Par 3 Golf Course in Miami Beach, Florida, admit that a prostitute once worked in a tree on the third hole. "She had a ladder nailed into the trunk of one of those big Banyan trees and a couple of four-by-eight sheets of plywood as a deck for her mattress," says an informed source. "She's gone, we dismantled her station—but she was there two years before we found her."

The question asked ever since at Bayshore: why hasn't play speeded up?

A dogleg par 3? What was the architect thinking?

A child's swing set, ten yards off the fairway? Was the designer insane?

Those crazy boulders in front of the green—what gives?

"It's the devil that makes us do that," says golf architect Bill Amick.

He means the client. A bad golf course often results from the struggle between a competent golf architect and whoever is paying the bills: the owner, the developer, the municipality.

"On a Florida site," Amick says, "I had already routed in about five water holes when the client came to me and said, 'More water.' So I added a couple more. He said, '*More* water.' He kept doing this till we wound up with about sixteen water holes. The man wanted water, and he couldn't see that the result was, shall we say, unbalanced."

Pete Dye credits a client for an embellishment that has since become synonymous with his style: railroad ties. Dye had seen railroad ties on the golf course at Prestwick, in Scotland, and had begun using them as bulkheads for elevated tees. Then he started work on a new course in Denver, on a site that had less than 90 acres to build on. "For some reason, the guy that hired me was enamored with railroad ties," Dye recalls. "When I arrived on the job, there were 30,000 of them out in the parking lot. So we used them on walkways and embankments, every place we could. Truly, if a course could have burned down, it was that one."

These stories recall the time the owner of Sotogrande in Spain, Joseph McMicking, lectured famed architect Robert Trent Jones on the Golden Rule. "I have the gold," McMicking said, "so I make the rules."

Housing developers, in particular, exert a diabolical influence on golf course design. For one thing, the developer usually sets aside all the prime pieces of ground for his houses, leaving the worst views and poorest terrain for the golf course. For another, the developer begrudges every acre he can't build on. "There's a sharp dogleg on the sixth hole of the Poipu Bay Resort course in Kauai," says Robert Trent Jones, Jr. "That came about because the owner pushed out the periphery of the housing and

Pete Dye's tee-on-stilts at the James River Golf Club, near Williamsburg, Virginia . (Copyright Bill Amick)

squeezed the course inward. The dogleg got sharper because that was the only way we could work it around an environmentally sensitive blind spider patch.

"The same thing happened in Chicago on a course called Crystal Tree. The owner was pushing me hard on bringing houses in close to the holes, and I kept pushing them back. The owners are my co-authors, as I like to say, but I like to make sure that they can write a little bit."

A more extreme example of client influence is Pete Dye's five-tiered green at the Carmel Valley Ranch Resort in Carmel, California. The putting surface stretches laterally from where Dye wanted to put the green to where the client wanted it. "What kind of golf shot is a ninety-yard putt that has to clamber up five levels?" asked *Golf* magazine.

Many architects blame their clients for the 1980s trend of courses with extreme mounding and sharp terracing of greens and bunkers—features that photograph beautifully at sunset when the long shadows add drama. "That one photograph in a glossy magazine might sell a hundred homesites or a couple of dozen memberships," says a well-known designer. "The trouble is, the golfers have to live with those unplayable features long after the photographer has departed."

And is there a client who doesn't want a signature hole? Cypress Point has its sixteenth over the water, Pebble Beach its eighteenth along the shore, the TPC at Sawgrass its island-green seventeenth. Shouldn't Wayward Hills have a volcano hole or something?

"I beg my clients not to ask me to build them an island green," says Rees Jones, brother of Jones, Jr., and acclaimed designer of Haig Point Golf Club and Atlantic Golf Club. "Successful golf courses are ones that have alternate routes of attack. When you build an island green, you merely create the intimidation factor, and half the players who play it think they can't hit the shot. I stand up on the seventeenth hole at the TPC, and I'm nervous as hell."

Yes, but blue water looks so nice next to green grass and black railroad ties. And if you can get the water to *move* . . .

"Waterfalls were all the rage for a while," says another architect. "Ted Robinson designs with a lot of water, and Jack Nicklaus did a nice one down in Texas with his Hills of Lakeway course. So now you've got people contriving waterfalls in the middle of Kansas."

The owner of Spanish Trail in Las Vegas, for example, decided he wanted a waterfall on the third hole of his Lakes Nine, but he didn't make his wishes known until the hole was half-built. The waterfall is there today—it's the owner's own design—but it partially blocks the view of the green. In another case, the Japanese owner of Desert Dunes in Palm Springs, California, decided to decorate his seventeenth green with a formal rock garden and a colonnade of saguaro cactuses imported from Arizona.

"That's the kind of thing that happens," says Jones, Jr. "You have one concept of golf, and the owner has another concept of decoration."

And remember, the architect does his job and moves on. The client stays behind with his checkbook, his course superintendent, and his own idea of what the course should look like.

"Ours is a form of art," Rees Jones notes wistfully, "where they can put a mustache on the *Mona Lisa*."

Worst Finish for Short Hitters: P. B. Dye's Cypress Course at the Palm Beach Polo Club, Wellington, Florida. The sixteenth is a 231-yard par 3, the seventeenth is a 641-yard par 5, the eighteenth is a 450-yard par 4, and all three holes play into a prevailing wind. Dye was obviously trying to protect par from the club's resident pro: 1992 Masters champion Fred Couples.

HAZY HILLS GOLF COURSE
Normal, Illinois
Par 35, 9 holes, 2,900 yards

"*Caddyshack* in the cornfields. . .a whacked-out whiffer's paradise. . .a true hacker's haven. . ."

So rhapsodized the *Chicago Tribune*, a few years ago, in a 1,600-word tribute to Hazy Hills Golf Course. Hazy Hills, a.k.a. "Crazy Hills" or "Crazy Hazy," was the course "where beer comes with your golf cart, where only the green is safe from stray shots, where birdies are rare and eagles don't dare." It was the course where a motorcycle gang, "tattooed, bearded, booted, and ready to kick par," roared in for a fast nine holes; where boozy church camp counselors launched wild shots through car windshields; where screwball duffers crashed their golf carts playing bumper car in the parking lot.

"Its owners sell tolerance," pealed the erudite *Tribune*, "—a sort of laissez fairways."

For some reason, the staff and golfers at Hazy Hills took this coverage as a less-than-total endorsement. "The owner and his wife—and *my* wife—didn't see the humor in it," says course manager Joe Ellenberger. "The story gave the impression that everybody was running around half-naked with a can of beer in hand." Adds pro-shop employee Joe Southwick: "It made us feel kind of foolish."

Then the story was a pack of lies?

"No, it wasn't inaccurate," says Ellenberger. "But the writer took something that happened maybe once a year and made you think it was an everyday occurrence."

The bumper-car thing, for instance. That only happened once, and Ellenberger handled it quietly, whacking one of the culprits across the back with a 3-iron. The motorcycle gang never came back, either—probably having found what they were looking for when they got to Chicago and played Medinah.

Still, there's no denying that Hazy Hills attracts a bunch of crooked shooters. Joe's son Tom, who was course superintendent until he chucked it for a job selling insurance in North Carolina, told the *Tribune* that at least one person in every foursome hit the clubhouse with a ball. "The only safe place on this course is on the green, next to the cup," said Tom, who shared the course record of 30 with his father. "I've had two windows knocked out of my car, and there are ball marks all over it."

The brains behind this shooting gallery is course owner and designer Ben Gildersleeve, a retired farmer and seed-company millionaire. Gildersleeve built the course seventeen years ago, running his tractors and mowers along the flood-prone Mackinaw River, 15 miles north of Bloomington-Normal. "It's pretty terrain, but it's wide open," says a golfer who has played Hazy Hills many times. "The fairways are five miles wide, and they all kind of run into each other. It's just a big, wide, hilly area where duffers can spray shots at each other."

The eighth hole at Hazy Hills, on the south end of the property, floods so regularly that it plays to different yardages, depending on the water level. Other holes sport out-of-bounds markers, although they are nowhere near the course boundary. "The stakes are just to penalize you for hitting into other fairways and tees," says our source. That very openness accounts for Hazy Hills's popularity with beginning golfers—the course logs up to

35,000 rounds a season—and explains why Gildersleeve hasn't hired a Jack Nicklaus or a Dan Maples to modify his design. "We don't have any sand, and we haven't planted any rough," says Joe Ellenberger. "It's still a wide-open golf course."

Wide-open in every sense of the word. Hazy Hills attracts senior golfers, teenagers on dates, happy-hour refugees, Japanese and American factory workers from a nearby automobile plant, students playing hooky from Southern Illinois University, and "retired farmers who've taken up golf as revenge against the land"—another *Tribune* quote.

"It didn't hurt us," Ellenberger says, referring to the newspaper's coverage. "We got people who drove all the way down from Chicago to play." It's even rumored that a golf writer for a national magazine is working on a coffee-table book about Hazy Hills. Working title: *Crazy Hazy—The Great Gildersleeve and His Contribution to Pasture Pool*.

Pretty heady stuff for a golf course that's close to Normal.

Although he did not win a Pulitzer Prize for his breakthrough reportage on Hazy Hills Golf Course, *Chicago Tribune* writer Wes Smith suffered the usual slings and arrows of high-profile journalism. "For a long time, I didn't go back to Hazy Hills, because I knew they were mad at me," says Smith, the paper's Midwest correspondent. "The local radio call-in shows chewed me up for a couple of days, and friends told me they heard talk in bars about what an ass that guy from the *Tribune* was."

Q: *So the reaction caught you by surprise?*

A: It did. You write stories where you think people are going to be offended, and they aren't. But I wrote *this* story thinking no one would be offended, and they were. The story angered the owner, Ben Gildersleeve. And I think the golf pro was mad at me, too—a little guy named Jake. He told me he couldn't stand to watch the people he gave lessons to, because he picked up too many bad habits.

Q: *Was Joe Ellenberger mad?*

A: Joe was not mad, and his son Tom thought the story was hilarious—he's sort of a mischief-maker. But Joe's wife, who I'm real fond of, was madder than hell at me.

J O H N   G A R R I T Y

And she was madder than hell at her son for telling me the stories. I guess it just sort of hurt her pride.

It's one of those stories that I really regretted writing.

Q: But it's clear that the story was poking gentle fun at Hazy Hills.

A: Actually, that golf course is near and dear to my heart. I worked in Bloomington—my first newspaper job out of college. A guy I lived with helped build Hazy Hills, and he kept telling me stories of the crazy people who went out there to learn how to play golf. So I went out there and played a few rounds. It's typical of golf courses that have a lot of farmers who have never played before. There's these little courses around Illinois that are just nothing but flat cow pasture with flags stuck in the ground.

Q: Hazy Hills is a bit more than a cow pasture, isn't it?

A: Yes, it shows evidence of design. I think Ben Gildersleeve is typical of a kind of successful man you find in the Midwest. He started a family seed company and ended up a millionaire when it got bought by one of the giant seed companies. So he entertained himself by building this golf course. And he sort of did it his way. I think he let Joe Ellenberger give him some direction, but he took it only grudgingly.

Q: Any quirks in the design?

A: Well, it's just so wide-open. At one time, there was a hole where he wanted you to hit over this big lake he'd built. But everybody cheated by going around it. Nobody would try to hit over the water, because nobody could. So he finally had to move the green across the water to bring it into play. He had to go with the will of the people.

Q: *What about the water hazard?*

A: They've dragged a lot of stuff out of that big main pond—golf bags and everything. You always hear these stories about golf courses, like the one where the guy throws his bag in a lake and has to come back later because his car keys are in the bag? I've heard that as a joke, but they swear it really happened at Hazy Hills.

Q: *Any chance that you'll play at Hazy Hills again?*

A: Well, I quit going there because everyone was mad at me. But a year or so ago, my friend was back in town, and he wanted to play. So he told Ben he was going to go out and play, and he added that I was going to play, too. And Ben said, "Oh yeah?"

But Ben gave us a free round, so I guess I'm forgiven.

Flagsticks often disappear from the greens at New York City's Van Cortlandt Park Golf Course, America's oldest public course. "We sometimes have to replace the one on the ninth green three or four times a day," head pro Bill Castner told New York *magazine. "But we've decided to just keep on doing it till every kid in the neighborhood has a flagstick on his bedroom wall."*

Castner got his street smarts when he was manager at La Tourette, another New York City course. One morning, the greenskeeper reported that someone had driven a car onto the first fairway during the night and set fire to it, leaving a smoldering hulk. Castner's calm advice: "Paint a white line around it and call it 'Ground Under Repair.'"

BAD TOURNAMENT COURSES:
A FOND RETROSPECTIVE

"Boy, if the pros had to play this goat ranch—"

Sound familiar? Well, from time to time the august names of golf *do* play courses that fall short of Pine Valley standards.

"They've had a bunch of raggedy old courses they've played on," says Associated Press golf writer Bob Green, who has covered the PGA Tour for twenty-five years. "Hartford had a pretty bad golf course. The one in Greensboro, where Sam Snead won all his tournaments, was not very good. Colonial, in Memphis, is now a parking lot. Montreal Municipal, the site of the Canadian Open, was a *real* bad golf course. The seventeenth green, a par three, had no grass on it and wouldn't hold a shot. It was darn near unplayable."

Graybeard pros still talk about Brackenridge Park Golf Course, a San Antonio muni that hosted the Texas Open most years from 1922 to 1959. Brackenridge had so much trouble growing grass on its tees that rubber mats were provided for the pros. Drought years brought dust storms. Biblical-plague years brought grasshoppers. "And the mud!" laughs former Tour star Bob Rosburg. "We used to steal knives from restaurants to scrape the mud off our shoes at Brackenridge." The 1955 champion, Mike Souchak, played his final round in below-freezing temperatures and shot a 65—with gloves on. Another year, the Open moved across town to Willow

JOHN GARRITY

Springs Golf Course, where players were allowed to tee up the ball in snow-covered fairways.

Another infamous tour stop was Burneyville, Oklahoma, home of the annual Waco Turner Open. The Burneyville course (since upgraded and renamed Falconhead Golf Course) was a hard, dusty piece of flatland bisected by an ugly ridge. Former touring pro Tom Garrity will never forget an early-morning practice round with Bobby Nichols at the 1961 tournament. "We got to the first green," Garrity says, "and there were wild onions growing on it. They weren't tiny tufts, either, but big onions, several inches high."

The host at Burneyville was Waco Turner, an eccentric oilman who sometimes livened things up by buzzing the golfers in his private plane. In addition to the men's tournament, he promoted an early LPGA event named for his wife: the Opie Turner Open. The golf course was so sunbaked for the Opie, writes golf historian Rhonda Glenn, that a committee of tour husbands had to pound the cups into the greens and leave them there for the entire week. But Turner made up for these shortcomings with his hospitality. When a player finished nine holes, she was ushered to an old junked Cadillac and towed to the tenth tee, some two miles away.

Burneyville was a lark for the ladies, but the Bayou Den Country Club in Beaumont, Texas, turned out to be a snake pit. The year was 1961. A week of heavy rain made the golf course unplayable for the Babe Zaharias Open, and the women were reduced to playing cards and ironing clothes. "For ten days, the players tried to finish the fifty-four-hole tournament," Glenn writes in *The*

Illustrated History of Women's Golf. "The golfers finally managed to complete their first rounds by playing nine holes, shotgun start, at 2 P.M., after wooden planks were laid on the soaked fairways to provide paths to the greens. Water moccasins wriggled everywhere."

As hazards go, venomous snakes rank right up there with Pete Dye's bunkers, so the lady pros were understandably jittery. Players yelled and waved to the groups behind, pointing out snakes. A caddy, cleaning a club in a pond, lifted it out of the water to find a baby moccasin curled around the shaft. One player found a dead snake with a golf ball in its mouth, and the eventual champion, Marilyn Smith, found a dead snake in a ball washer.

"Candy Phillips and I had a lengthy discussion concerning what we would do if we missed one green with our wedge shots," said Mary Lou Crocker. "Candy decided to withdraw if she missed the green because she wasn't going to walk anywhere except on those planks."

You don't find courses like that on today's tours. The tournament standard, heading into the twenty-first century, is a lush, manicured sward along the lines of the Muirfield Village Golf Club in Dublin, Ohio, which Dan Jenkins once described as "in such immaculate condition that people would sooner have dropped cigarette butts on their babies' tummies."

But while golf courses and maintenance have gotten better, the touring pros have grown more irascible. When the TPC at Sawgrass opened in 1982, J. C. Snead denounced it as "ninety percent horse manure and ten percent luck," and John Mahaffey asked, "If you birdie the eighteenth hole, do you win a free game?" La Purisma Golf Club drew similar flak in its first year of action at the LPGA's Santa Barbara Open. Frustrated by high winds, small greens, tight fairways, and tough hazards, the players dubbed the inland course "La Prisona." And when Poppy Hills replaced spectacular Cypress Point in the rota of the AT&T Pro-Am at Pebble Beach, former U.S. Open champ Johnny Miller quipped, "It's like replacing Bo Derek with Roseanne Barr."

The so-called great courses have taken their hits, too. The legendary Sam Snead ridiculed the equally legendary Merion East course, as well as the fabled Old Course at St. Andrews, in Scotland. Fuzzy Zoeller and Gary Player blasphemed the greens at sacred Augusta National. Larry Ziegler facetiously praised the greens at Harbour Town Golf Links, saying, "They're so bumpy the gallery can't tell when I have the yips."

No one can pinpoint when all this grousing got started, but the turning point was probably the 1952 U.S. Open, won by Ben Hogan at Oakland Hills Country Club in suburban Detroit. The course had been remodeled for the Open by Robert Trent Jones, and when Hogan staggered in with his winning 292—7-over par—he said, "I am glad to have brought this monster to its knees."

The famous quip made Jones's reputation and ushered in the era of the high-profile golf architect. It also altered forever the relationship between the golfer and the golf course. Henceforth, the land would speak to the golfer through a malevolent interpreter—the "demon architect."

A few years later, Jones was again at the center of

controversy when Hazeltine Golf Club in Chaska, Minnesota, one of his original designs, hosted the 1970 Open. Jack Nicklaus criticized what he thought was an excess of blind holes. ("Maybe Nicklaus is blind," Jones shot back.) Dave Hill said, "If I had to play this course every day for free, I'd find another game." Hill also said, "They ruined a good farm when they built this course."

"I'm not a fiend, I don't hate golfers," Jones insisted. But the tournament players—who had not yet met Pete Dye—thought otherwise. They groused that Jones's courses were too long, his greens too contoured, his penalties too severe. Lee Trevino played a round at California's Spyglass Hill and said, "They ought to hang the man who designed this course. Ray Charles could have done better."

"Golfers complain a lot," Jones observed.

Today, the brunt of the tournament players' opprobrium falls on Dye and on one of their own, Jack Nicklaus. When Dye pulled the sheet off his TPC at Sawgrass in 1982, the greens were so severe that Tom Watson asked, "Is it against the rules to carry a bulldozer in your bag?" And when tournament winner Jerry Pate threw Dye and himself into the lake on the eighteenth hole, *Golf World* noted that a few of the watching pros "were hoping that the water was ten feet deep and neither could swim. Especially Dye."

The main complaint about Nicklaus is that he designs like Dye. "Nicklaus's approach to green design is almost sadistic," says veteran touring pro Frank Beard. "You stand there in the fairway with a six-iron in your hand and you look at the pin, and you realize you've got about twenty feet of green and a yawning bunker on either side.

JOHN GARRITY

Twenty feet—that's not much for a six-iron. And these bunkers are straight down." Tour star Paul Azinger played a casual round at the Nicklaus-designed Renegade course at the Desert Mountain Golf Club in Carefree, Arizona, and shot 82. "But that course was unplayable," Azinger said with a laugh.

Clearly, the tournament pros have more than aesthetics on their minds when they make such criticisms. "Where the players really complain," says architect Rees Jones, "is when there are features on golf courses that penalize a slightly errant shot severely, and they get a double bogey instead of a par and shoot themselves out of a tournament."

That must be it. Give the average pro the choice between a wheelbarrow full of water moccasins and a new Jack Nicklaus course, and the pro will take the snakes every time.

> "Do the architects realize how much we hate the new courses?"
>
> —*Paul Azinger, touring pro*

STONE HARBOR GOLF COURSE
Cape May Court House, New Jersey
Par 72, 6,950 yards

Nearest museum: You're walking on it, stupid

"Y ou didn't like Stone Harbor?" The pale guy in the black turtleneck looks at you in disbelief. "Well, obviously you didn't *understand* it!"

Welcome to the world of Desmond Muirhead, the only architect who designs golf courses the way Ingmar Bergman filmed movies—through a glass, darkly. "Muirhead's bag is symbolism," writes *Golf Digest*'s Ron Whitten. "To him, an elevated tee isn't just an elevated tee—it's a symbol of the American male's desire to regain the position of world dominance lost in Vietnam."

As we all know, one man's symbol is another man's enigma. When it opened in 1989, Stone Harbor immediately came to represent architectural self-indulgence. Built on top of a flat and bleak publinx course, the new private track reflected a brilliant mind driven to feverish extremes. Muirhead, playing with clay like God, threw down an island green, island bunkers, an island fairway, a tree growing in the middle of a fairway, a tree growing out of a green, a bunker on stilts, a green shaped like New Jersey—a delirium dreamscape of sand, turf, and water. Little wonder that Whitten called Stone Harbor "the most contrived course I've ever seen."

The most famous hole was number 7, a par 3 known as "Jaws" (see page 36). The Stone Harbor membership, made up of guys and gals who would rather watch *Lethal Weapon IV* than an Andy Warhol movie, sent the bulldoz-

J O H N   G A R R I T Y

ers after it in 1991. But Stone Harbor was, and is, much more than Jaws. "Muirhead outdid himself down there," says agronomist John DeMatteo. "I played it once, and if he hadn't put all that crazy stuff in, I'd have enjoyed it, because it was a nice-playing golf course. It had difficulty to it, it had a couple of really good holes on it. But. . . but. . ." DeMatteo's voice catches, in the manner of people who have seen horrific things or been snatched by aliens in flying saucers.

The overall theme of Stone Harbor is mythology. Jaws was a reworking, in water, sand, and turfgrass, of Jason and the Argonauts. A bunker behind another green represents Pandora's box. The par-3 number 17 is Medusa's head, with bunkers forming the snakes. Another hole is shaped like a lion, although, as one critic notes, "you can't tell it's a lion unless you're about a thousand feet off the ground." The ninth hole, since modified, had a green in the shape of New Jersey, guarded by a bunker shaped like Pennsylvania. "Why do the whole thing in mythology and then put the state of New Jersey in there?" asks a bewildered DeMatteo. "Does that make sense?"

Probably not, and so New Jersey came out, as did the sword and helmet on number 10 and several wooden bulkheads that members said bent and broke their clubs. "We kind of kept the changes low profile for a number of reasons," says Stone Harbor president and developer Gordon Shaffner. "Desmond sent some proteges to hear the members' complaints about the Jaws hole, and he did a fantastic job with the redesign. It's still basically a Desmond Muirhead course; we've just rolled back the rough edges."

So there you are, standing on the tee at the par-3 fourth, getting a little queasy as you look down on a bathtub-like depression filled with troughs and mounds and moon craters. The craters represent: A) spent thunderbolts hurled at Pegasus by Zeus; B) doors to the Minotaur's labyrinth; C) laundry baskets left on the Plain of Archimedes by Euripides.

The answer is A, but this is hardly what is meant by "a good test of golf."

You don't have to own a helicopter to conclude that Stone Harbor is over most people's heads.

The Norseman hole at Stone Harbor——a Desmond Muirhead hole deserving of a Viking funeral. (Copyright Ron Whitten)

Forbes *magazine reports that country singer Kenny Rogers built his own golf course on his 1,200-acre estate in Colbert, Georgia. It started as a simple practice hole for the golf-crazy Rogers, and now it's a full-size eighteen-hole layout with "waterfalls, brooks, and bridges."*

Rogers designed it himself, and sometimes he screwed up. "For example, his sixteenth and seventeenth holes had improper drainage. After every heavy rain, fish from the ponds would wash up on the greens." Rogers, an eleven handicapper, put in a complex system of drains and pumps to manage the brooks and ponds. "If you design a golf course yourself," he said, "you have to expect to go through some catastrophes."

The weirdest feature at Rogers Yard Golf Club was the foliage, which tended to wander. Rogers bought a hydraulic tree mover and, like most kids with a new toy, he couldn't leave it alone. "Sometimes when I'm playing a hole I'll realize where I want a tree," Rogers said. "So I'll tell my men, and later, when I come back that afternoon, there will be a new tree in the middle of the fairway."

As this book went to press, the about-to-be-divorced Rogers was involved in a bitter custody battle over the golf course and tree mover.

"When I think of Angelenos beating balls on bare mats at Rancho Park while waiting two hours just so they can play a miserable six-hour round of golf on putting greens that are better suited for feeding livestock, I don't understand it."
—Rex Pickett, California Golfer

There's an old saw that goes, "A bad day on the golf course is better than a good day at the office." That is certainly true, and the author concedes that great fun can be had playing bad golf courses. In fact, some of the courses in this volume are more fun to play than the layouts you find in the Great Golf Course books.

But it doesn't change the fact that these courses are bad. Otherwise, what would be the point of the golf magazines' annual lists of World's 100 Greatest Courses, World's Greatest Resort Courses, America's Best New Courses, America's Best Courses Ranked by State, America's Best Public Courses, and Best Southern Semi-Private Courses? These best lists are trumpeted in the press releases and sales pitches of every course architect skilled enough to be ranked. And if these courses are "great," other courses have to be "near-great," "good," "okay," "mediocre"—all the way down to "shabby," "putrid," and "staggeringly inept."

So how does a golf course get to be bad?

"It can happen years after the architect has left the site," says one course designer. "But most of the time, it's the architect's fault."

This comes as no surprise. After all, when a golf course turns out well, the architect steps forward and modestly points out that he was merely following "the principles of good golf course design."

But when a golf course turns out poorly, the archi-

JOHN GARRITY

Bad maintenance can always take up where bad design falters.
(Copyright John DeMatteo)

tect—if he can be found at all—mumbles that the site was unworkable, the owner a fool, and the contractor a drunk. Never do we hear the architect forthrightly admit that he adhered to the "principles of bad golf course design."

When, obviously, he did.

Where do you go to learn the principles of bad golf course design? Oddly enough, you don't go to the bad golf course designer. His grasp of bad design is strictly intuitive, and any questions you ask him will merely bring a look of dismay to his normally untroubled face.

A better way to understand bad design is to go to a successful golf architect and pose the question: "If you were *trying* to build a bad golf course, how would you go

AMERICA'S WORST GOLF COURSES

about it?" This produces a moment's confusion, because talented designers aren't accustomed to thinking inversely. But once they grasp the idea, the top architects are veritable founts of bad advice.

Robert Trent Jones, Jr., for instance, has this tip for the would-be bad architect: "Don't believe any instruments; only believe your eye."

He elaborates: "There are a lot of dead pilots on mountains who didn't believe their instruments, and there are a lot of bad golf courses because the architect worked by eye. Somebody says, 'That looks level,' and he goes with it. A year later, you putt your ball at the Cheyenne Mountain Broadmoor, and the ball falls off the mountain.

"Similarly, you may think thirty paces is ninety feet, but maybe you've gotten a little older, and now it's only eighty feet. If you're placing sprinkler heads, that's bad. The system won't water everything."

Another suggestion from Jones: hire unproven contractors. "Bulldozer operators are notorious for having big machines and small knowledge of the game."

So right there, you have two principles: (1) Work without instruments; and (2) Hire an unproven contractor.

MORE BAD ADVICE FROM GOOD ARCHITECTS . . .

T om Fazio, the widely acclaimed designer of Shadow Creek, Barton Creek, and, if you've got ten or fifteen million dollars, Your Creek: (3) "The bad golf course has lots of blind shots, holes where you hit over the tops of hills. The green is down at the bottom, beyond the hill, and you can't play until the guys on the other side ring a bell. Then you hit to a space in the air. There's a lot of golf holes like that in the Northeast, where the terrain is severe and there's underground rock and they used to build golf courses with horses and scrapes." (4) "I'd say a golf hole with multiple cross hazards is not good design for modern holes. Of course, you find such holes on nationally known courses." (5) "Personally, I don't like uphill par-three holes, although I've seen some great ones. That's just not my idea of a good par three."

Golfplan's Ron Fream, designer of the twenty-seven-hole Eurodisney, outside Paris, and golf architect to the Sultan of Brunei: (6) "When you're selecting grasses, just pick a box off the shelf. Some architects do that, you know. They use whatever they're sold or whatever the commission justifies. It's green and it's grass, but it's not as green or as good as it should be because it's the wrong grass. And if it's the wrong grass for the climate, it will turn into weeds." (7) "You can do a lot of mischief with bad drainage. One nice touch is to build tees that drain to the front, into the line of play. That way, all the water collects where the golfers have to walk. You can also design the greens so that all the water drains off in front, where the tractors have to drive and the golfers walk up." (8) "Concave fairways are another good mud producer. Remember, any time you're walking through water on a golf course, the soil underneath is liquid. As it dries, it becomes plastic, compounding the compaction problem. And compaction is like cancer on a golf course."

Dr. Michael Hurdzan, past president of the American Society of Golf Course Architects (ASGCA) and designer of 150 golf courses, including Canada's Devil's Pulpit Golf Course: (9) "Tilt the tee to the front to help the average golfer slice the ball even more, and then bolster the effect by building a prodigious left-to-right tilt into the fairway." (10) "Tighten the playing areas with trees. Nothing complicates golf like trees—the old Scots called them 'sand traps in the sky.' " (11) "Fill your sand bunkers with small, round-particle sand—like itty-bitty buckshot—to ensure fried-egg lies. I have seen balls enter a bunker and disappear before my eyes." (12) "Install bahia grass rough or some other inescapable, wrist-jarring substitute. Buffalo grass, tall fescue, or bentgrass will work."

Bill Amick, another past president of the ASGCA and designer of Perdido Bay, Mangrove Bay, and Pelican Bay: (13) "Build the course in a housing subdivision with huge distances between the holes to discourage walking." (14) "Line both sides of every hole with houses and back yards. Cursing and club-throwing golfers mingling with shouting homeowners and crying kids—the American Dream!" (15) "Design the course with the assistance of a touring pro. He's sure to have the technical training and the time between tournaments to improve your crude design." (16) "Build par threes that golfers—especially women—can't reach with their tee shots. The ideal par three is a two hundred-thirty-yarder to an island green." (17) "Design for the photographer, not the golfer." (18) "Make all the par fours side-by-side, down-and-back holes. This gives the golfer the comfort of feeling he's always on the same hole." (19) "Design as many forced carries as possible, to prey on the minds of short hitters, beginners, and wimps." (20) "Give your course four par fives of similar length, requiring the same type shots, all headed in the same direction. Back-to-back par fives with these qualities are even better." (21) "Design your par fives so that long hitters can reach the green in two without difficulty, but short hitters must always take three. This gives an automatic four-stroke advantage to long hitters before anyone tees off." (22) "Frame the fairways with extreme mounding. These artificial Alps will be forever expensive to maintain because they will require hand mowing." (23) "Make the sand bunkers deep and steep with frivolous outlines. The function of sand on a golf course is to dazzle and be photographed." (24) "Install cart paths where they will be most visible. Cart paths are the most important part of a modern golf course, so all paths should be in play and, for beauty's sake, in full view." (25) "After construction, make changes without consulting the architect. The greens committee chairman should remove any bunkers or trees that don't suit his game." (26) "Encourage the maintenance crew to ignore the original outlines when mowing the greens and fairways. Straight fairway outlines are easier to mow than those with unnecessary curves." (27)

"Reverse the order of the nines. This should be done without considering the difficulty of the beginning or finishing holes, the orientation of the holes to the sun or prevailing winds, the traffic patterns of golfers to and from the nines, or any other consideration taken into account by the golf course architect in originally numbering the holes."

If all else fails, Amick says, a bad golf course can be achieved simply by (28) "resisting remodeling. No tees or bunkers should ever be moved, even though the best men golfers now hit a golf ball twenty percent or thirty percent farther than their predecessors." The no-remodeling principle, he adds, "is easiest to implement if a golf architect of note is rumored to have designed the course."

Oddly enough, none of the architects interviewed mentioned site selection as a prerequisite for bad golf course design. While it is true that a bad designer can screw up a beautiful site, certain terrains just lend themselves to bad outcomes. Mountainsides, for instance. Unless the owner of a mountain golf course is prepared to spend huge sums on cut-and-fill operations, the course will be susceptible to massive erosion during rainfall. Mountain courses also suffer from unwalkability, hard-to-read greens, and cold mountain shadows.

The bad architect also has friends in low places. Floodplains pose the problems of poor drainage, soil compaction, and. . .yeah, flooding. Rocky soil leads to high construction costs and dangerous playing conditions. Airport locations are noisy. Arctic conditions produce permafrost, reindeer droppings, and sunless days. Environmentally sensitive sites force the architect to detour around obscure, endangered species. Swampland can be infested with snakes and Cajun fiddlers.

Other sites, as the courses in this volume demonstrate, are simply "too something"—too hot (Furnace Creek), too small (Plantation), too flat (half the courses in Illinois), too exposed to adjacent development (Z-Boaz), or too close to Donald Trump (Mar A Lago, Palm Beach, Florida).

All these shortcomings can be summed up in Principle 29: Build in a bad place.

The bad golf course designer must also consider the Alister Mackenzie Inverse Principles. Mackenzie was the English physician who designed some of the world's greatest courses, including Royal Melbourne, Augusta National, and Cypress Point. In the 1920s, Mackenzie published a list of "essential features of an ideal golf course." This list, reprinted many times, consists of pithy injunctions such as, "Every hole should have a different character" and "There should be a minimum of blindness for the approach shots." Taken as a whole, Mackenzie's list is a sort of Thirteen Commandments of good golf course design. It follows, then, that a list of bad design principles can be derived simply by reversing Mackenzie at every point. To wit (and with already-stated principles omitted):

THE ALISTER MACKENZIE INVERSE PRINCIPLES:

(30) The course, where possible, should *not* be arranged in two loops of nine holes.

(31) There should *not* be a large proportion of good two-shot holes, two or three drive-and-pitch holes, and at least four one-shot holes.

(32) There should be *much* walking between the greens and tees, and the course should be arranged so there is *never* a slight walk forwards from the green to the next tee; then the holes are *not* sufficiently elastic to be lengthened in the future if necessary.

(33) The greens and fairways should be *flat and featureless*, but there should be *considerable* hill climbing.

(34) Every hole should have the *same* character.

(35) The course should have *unattractive* surroundings, and all the artificial features should have so *contrived* an appearance that a stranger is *able* to distinguish them from nature *at a glance*.

(36) There should be *no* variety in the strokes required to play the various holes—viz., interesting brassy shots, iron shots, pitch and runup shots.

(37) There should be a *perpetual presence* of the annoyance and irritation caused by the necessity of searching for lost balls.

(38) The course should be so *dull* that even the plus man is *disinclined* to improve his game in attempting shots he has hitherto been unable to play.

(39) The course should be so arranged that the long handicap player, or even the absolute beginner, will be unable to enjoy his round *because* of the fact that he is piling up a big score.

(40) The course should *not* be equally good during winter and summer, the texture of the greens and fairways should be

imperfect, and the approaches should *not* have the same consistency as the greens.

Have we exhausted the subject? Hardly. A bad golf course can be made worse by. . .

(41) Aligning the opening holes into the rising sun and the closing holes into the setting sun.
(42) Routing holes in a counter-clockwise direction around the perimeter of the property. Most golfers slice their tee shots, so a strict diet of out-of-bounds on the right slows play and inflates handicaps.
(43) Positioning tees and greens in dangerous proximity.
(44) Building steep-faced bunkers that can only be entered from one side, requiring extensive raking.
(45) Building sloping tees—the most exquisite result being a slightly downhill, hanging lie with out-of-bounds on the right.
(46) Ignoring prevailing wind conditions.
(47) Placing tees in heavily shaded areas where grass won't grow.
(48) Aligning the practice range so that mis-hit balls will stray onto adjoining fairways.
(49) Planting 150-yard stakes or bushes at random distances from the centers of greens.
(50) Routing cart paths so far from the fairways that the golfer walks more from his cart to his ball than he would have walked carrying his bag.

. . .and so on. Considerations of space prevent a complete listing, but interested readers are invited to write the author, who will read the entire list of 272 principles, over the phone, for a fee.

"Ron Fream," says an admiring colleague, "has made himself something of an expert on how *not* to do it."

If that sounds like less-than-faint praise for the international golf course architect, it's probably because the CEO and chief designer for Golfplan hasn't taken his slide show to your town yet. Fream lectures on the subject of golf course design blunders. His talk—"Build It Right the First Time"—is a virtual catalog of architectural ineptitude and malfeasance witnessed in his almost three decades as an architect in fifty countries. Although best known for his designs in Europe and Asia, Fream still works in the States; his Redhawk Golf Course and Oakhurst Country Club were selected by *California Golf* magazine as the two best new courses in California for 1991.

We talked to him anyway.

Q: *Where do golf courses go wrong?*

A: It can happen in any of three areas—on the drawing board, during construction, or after the fact because of maintenance practices. Poor design is not as common as it used to be because there are more American-trained architects traveling the world now, talented architects. But there are problems that come up all the time because of inadequate construction.

JOHN GARRITY

Q: *For instance?*

A: Sometimes developers and contractors needlessly cut down trees. Or they kill trees by accident. There may be a shady spot, and they'll park the trucks and bulldozers there while they eat lunch or dinner. All that traffic can compact the soil and cause a tree to die. Or I've seen where they work on the engines in the shade, because it's cooler there, and they dump transmission fluid or oil on the ground within the tree's drip line. The tree dies. It's a little thing, but that one tree, five or ten years from now, could make all the difference in how the hole plays.

Q: *Is it a question of incompetence, or is it usually the case of an owner cutting corners?*

A: It can be either. Somebody will come in and build all the bunkers six inches deep, shallow enough that you can putt out of them. Obviously, that destroys whatever design integrity the bunker had.

In other cases, it's just foolish cost-cutting. There's been talk lately that we need more golf courses that can be built for a million dollars, so more people can play golf. That's an absolute mistake. You can't build a decent course for a million, and if you do, you're going to spend any profits you make repairing the course later. There is a bottomline budget, which varies from site to site. If you don't spend money on proper seed beds and sound agronomic procedures, you're cutting your own throat.

Q: *These are the root causes of muddy bunkers and dusty tees?*

A: Sure. Not putting drainage into bunkers is a problem you see a lot. You get into the rainy season, and the course can be severely damaged. Tees that are too small, tees built out of local dirt instead of a seedbed mixture—that eventually leads to bare dirt tees that are ugly and uncomfortable to hit from. Greens built with local sand, because it's cheaper or because they just don't know any better, can lead to tremendous problems later.

So often I've seen a course where they strip all the topsoil off and put it into mounds along the fairway, leaving the underlying clay or heavy silt soil, or whatever the miserable stuff is. They leave *that* to grow the grass in, without modifying it or ameliorating it or putting on sand. You're supposed to grow grass in this junk? It's a horrible problem and very expensive to correct.

Q: *What about maintenance?*

A: If you want problems, just hire someone who's little more than a gardener, who's cheap, and who knows nothing about golf. There's a recipe for disaster! You create a visually beautiful green with all these contours and convolutions, and then some superintendent comes in and lets his crew mow them round. The superintendent doesn't notice these changes, because they are subtle and gradual, but in two or three years the greens are all round. You've lost the visual beauty and maybe some of the pin placements. An architect like Tom Fazio tries hard to do scenic things with bunkers—shapes, forms, configurations that look good. If a superintendent comes in and cuts the noses off those bunkers and turns them into circles, you got problems.

J O H N   G A R R I T Y

Q: How do you prevent that from happening?

A: We try to get around that by designing our greens with mounds and hollows placed so as to force the shape of the green. The guy mowing the green has to drive around them. That helps keep some of the shapes.

I should point out that a dedicated, college-trained superintendent can cover up the mistakes of an incompetent architect or contractor. A good super can overcome soil problems. He can tinker with the irrigation or add a few more heads. He can build another tee. He can take dirt out and put sand down, maybe put in a drainage line. You can have flat fairways and round, flat greens, and the super can fool you completely by growing brilliant grass and by shaping visually appealing greens with his mowers. A good super can take a goat track of a course and make it into something nice.

But you get somebody who doesn't know what he's doing, and it doesn't matter how good the design is—it's going to deteriorate.

Q: Sometimes, though, it's the design itself that's at fault.

A: Absolutely. Many of the fundamental problems start in the office, on the drawing board. Whatever is not addressed in the office—saline soils, alkaline soils, annual rainfall, typhoons, wind storms—will come back to haunt you in construction. Or worse, after you've opened for play. It's important that the architect, while designing, thinks about maintenance. He can't just worry about how to play a four-wood or a pitch shot to the green. He has to worry about growing grass and providing proper drainage.

AMERICA'S WORST GOLF COURSES

Q: *Are all architects qualified to do that?*

A: Unfortunately, no. Some architects don't know the difference between clay and sand. They're beautiful designers, great graphic artists, but they don't know how to make things grow.

Many guys call themselves golf architects these days. A lot of them play golf better than I do, and people tend to be impressed with a pro or a scratch player.

Q: *What are the most common design blunders?*

A: Lakes in the wrong place. Designing lakes, streams, and other terminal hazards without thinking about how they affect play, just putting them there because they look nice. Designing for the scratch player or pro, and forgetting the sixty-five-year-old lady on the par-five hole who's hitting her seventh shot to the green and doesn't need a lake in the way. Too often, we penalize the wrong golfers, the high handicappers, because we forget about them in the design process.

Blind shots. They were unavoidable in the days before modern earthmoving equipment, but blind hazards are no longer acceptable. You shouldn't hit what you think is a good tee shot and find your ball has gone in a hidden lake.

Q: *Is technical facility, by itself, enough to prevent a bad golf course?*

A: No. You still find architects that design with a rubber stamp: eighteen greens that look alike, each with a bunker on each side at the front edge; every fairway flat with the bunkers always two hundred twenty to two hundred thirty yards off the tee; every bunker oval or peanut-shaped. Monotonous! It's a severe problem that so many courses are just so boring.

Other architects design too much for their own egos. They've built this image of self-importance, or their marketing men have built them up to be the best, so they try to come in with a course that has the eighteen toughest greens in the world, or whatever. They can't build something the ladies like or the average golfer likes—it would threaten their manhood. It's got to be the pro that likes it and nobody else.

And you've always got the problem of the gold-plated golf course. Clients looking for prestige will hire a Nicklaus, a Jones, or one of the other famous architects. They're bound to spend a lot of money, but putting a famous name on it doesn't guarantee you either an efficient project or one that will make money in the long run. Some of the most expensive and most-publicized courses are now running into bankruptcy. Five years ago, they were monuments to somebody's brilliance; now they just look like monuments to somebody's open checkbook.

Worst cart-path ride between holes? Some say it's at the Carmel Valley Ranch Resort in Carmel, California—the ten-minute drive up a switchback trail from the tenth green to the eleventh tee. However, when you get to the top you have a spectacular view of the valley, plus you get to ask the robed guru the meaning of life.

No, the worst cart passage is in Missouri at Springfield's Deer Lake Country Club: a 300-yard journey under Interstate 44 through an old cattle tunnel. "It's only six feet high and about four feet wide," says architect Bill Amick. "We scratched our heads, wondering if golfers would go through such a long, dark tunnel. But it was the only way we could get to the six holes on the south side of the property."

Hey, golf itself can be a long, dark tunnel.

JOHN GARRITY

PARADISE VALLEY GOLF COURSE
St. Louis, Missouri

Par 70, 6,185 yards
Course rating: 68.2; slope: 112
Dominant aroma: Stable smells from adjacent horse farm
Special rules: "Ball striking power lines on number fifteen or number sixteen may be replayed without penalty."

"This half of road maintained by St. Louis County," reads a sign near the entrance to Paradise Valley. It's a fitting introduction to a golf course that specializes in half measures—half a practice range, half an idea of where it's going, and, in dry weather, half covered with grass. "It's a dust bowl," says a nationally known golf photographer who lives in St. Louis. "Dust tees, dust fairways. I look for a little bitty weed on the tees, something green to tee up on. By the end of the day, your shoes are covered with dust."

Actually, Paradise Valley enjoys a lovely setting. Wooded ridges conceal the nearby Chrysler Assembly Plant, and a creek meanders through the property. In autumn, the golf course offers an enchanting palette of fall colors. The problem is not the terrain, but a dearth of imagination. The signature hole is the 128-yard ninth, an absolutely flat par 3 with no hazards and a pin set in the center of a large, perfectly level green. The hole's name: "Deception."

Unfortunately, you can't hold a golfer's interest with irony alone. The fairways here open up generously off the tee—so generously as to be undefined. Here and there a bulldozer has shaped a few mounds as hazards,

AMERICA'S WORST GOLF COURSES

The baffling "Deception" par 3 at Paradise Valley Golf Club.
(John Garrity, Copyright 1993)

but the mounds are pathetically artificial. Play is heavy, nonetheless, especially on summer afternoons when league golfers take over the course. Long hitters will get a kick out of the Paradise Valley practice range, which disappears into the forest about 200 yards out. It's great sport trying to knock squirrels and blue jays off the branches.

(A note of caution: A few years back, the Chrysler plant was the site of an odometer-rollback scandal in which executives drove cars around for months before shipping them to dealers as "new." No big deal, but if you're playing a big-money match at Paradise Valley you might ask your opponent to count his strokes out loud and keep his scorecard in ink.)

Paradise Valley: it's not half-bad.

The poorest tee shot in golf? Architect Tom Fazio nominates the eighth at Pebble Beach Golf Links, a blind drive up a featureless hill with a hidden cliff at the end of the landing area. "Of course," Fazio says, "the second shot, off the cliff to that gorgeous green, is one of the greatest shots in golf."

FAIRBANKS GOLF AND COUNTRY CLUB
Fairbanks, Alaska

9 holes, par 29, 1,785 yards

Previous land use: Cryogenic test site

"Yeah, I've played it," says a recent visitor to America's frostiest golf course. "Pitiful."

His chilly assessment will surprise no one who has ever tried to build a golf course on permafrost. Turfgrass on permafrost (a frozen subsoil that hardens and softens with changes in temperature) yields a surface something like the cake portion of an ice-cream-cake roll. Over time, the fairways heave, turf buckles, topsoil crenelates, and you wind up with what *Sports Illustrated* once called "the most treacherous fairways imaginable."

A tee shot at Fairbanks *can* bounce forward; more likely, the ball will kick sideways upon landing, or nestle in clumpy grass, or wedge itself into a crack in the earth. "Or a fairway selection may collapse"—this, again, from *SI*. "Just such a mishap once dropped the club tractor and its driver into a hole twelve feet down and twenty feet long."

That being said, consider this: Fairbanks golfers complain mostly about their greens.

Okay, you're not going to get greens that register twelve on the Stimpmeter—not 165 miles from the Arctic Circle, anyway. But Fairbanks got by for years with oiled sand greens. Progress intervened, unfortunately, and now Alaska's pale golfers have to negotiate artificial-turf greens laid over concrete. "It's miniature golf without the windmills," says Rich Griffis, sports editor of the

J O H N   G A R R I T Y

Daily News-Miner. "Hit a green on the fly and you're dead meat," confirms Fairbanks city councilman Bob Eley. "It'll bounce like a baseball on Astroturf."

Consequently, Fairbanks members keep the ball low—so low that a shout of "Fore!" sends members hopping instead of ducking. "If you hit grounders," says Eley, "you can do pretty well on this course."

And if you're carrying a hunting rifle, you can maybe score something bigger than a birdie. Bears have been known to drag golf bags into the spruce forest, and a moose once glared angrily at a golfer who interrupted his grazing with a shot off the antlers.

Such are the trials of golf in Alaska, the most under-golfed state in the Union. The 1992 Yearbook of the United States Golf Association listed only eight member clubs for Alaska, and the golf season is so short that the entire state records fewer than a 100,000 rounds a year—less than some sunbelt courses clock in a season. "That's because it's cold in Alaska," says. . .well, never mind who said it.

But Fairbanks Golf & Country Club is rudimentary, even by Yukon standards. "The father of one of our staffers came up from Connecticut and was used to playing on country club courses," says *Daily News-Miner* sportswriter Bob Eley (yeah, it's the same guy). "He was pretty baffled by it all." The club rewards visiting golfers with its "Greens Badge of Courage"—a decoration meriting respect somewhere between that of the Croix de Guerre and the "You May Be a Winner" letter from Lake Pipeline Estates.

Mercifully, the golf course is dormant most of the year, demand dropping, as it does, during the two-hour, thirty-below-zero days of winter. Golf season stretches from May to September, when the days are long—endless, actually—and temperatures reach the sixties or higher. The day to mark on your calendar is June 19, when there is just enough light between 3 and 5 A.M. to permit 24-hour golf.

And remember—hit it low.

There are no elephants buried in the greens at Burning Tree Golf Club in Newark, Ohio, but a crew working on the fourteenth fairway in 1991 dug up an 11,000-year-old mastodon. Paleontologists cut into the giant creature's intestinal tract and found the mastodon's last meal—leafy stuff and grasses from some prehistoric halfway house—and teeming bacteria, the oldest living organisms yet discovered.

Signs at Burning Tree that used to say "Replace All Divots" now read "Report All Excavations."

PGA WEST STADIUM COURSE
La Quinta, California

Par 72, 7,260 yards

Previous land use: An innocent desert. Never harmed anybody

Curious fact: Course is on Golf Digest's list of "America's 100 Greatest Golf Courses"

There's an old "Monty Python" sketch in which a character responds to insistent questioning by saying, "I wasn't expecting the Spanish Inquisition"—only to have the door thrown open by a red-robed Torquemada who bellows, "*Nobody* expects the Spanish Inquisition!"

A round at PGA West's Stadium Course—a few holes, even—is a little like that. The names of the holes suggest the ingenious tortures Pete Dye has devised: "Black Hole," "Moat," "Eternity," "Sand Pit," "Alcatraz." But the names don't really do the holes justice. This desert layout is widely regarded as the most difficult golf course in the world (course rating 77.3, slope 151). It is the place where golfers start a round with a dozen new golf balls and stop by the pro shop after nine holes to buy a dozen more. It is the place where golfers make so many *X*s that the scorecard looks like a game of tic-tac-toe.

"You play PGA West to atone for your sins," says a well-known golf writer. "Nobody plays it for fun."

Need convincing? Hunker down on any of a hundred spectator mounds and watch for fifteen minutes. Here's a typical foursome, teeing off on number 10, a par 4 with forced carries over water from the tee and again from the fairway, and with water the length of the hole on the left.

Player 1: splash. Player 2: splash. Player 3: fairway. Player 4: wide right in grassy dunes.

On to their second shots. Player 1 drops a ball and swings for the green: splash. Player 2 drops a ball and tops it into the water. Player 3, from the fairway, hooks his ball into the water. Player 4, from the right rough, skulls one to the edge of the water and *then* dumps it into the drink, attempting to pitch to the green. Number of balls in water for the hole: six.

A short stroll takes us to the island-green seventeenth, the hole Lee Trevino aced for $175,000 in the 1987 Skins Game. From the tournament tee, on a high bluff 166 yards from the flag, a portly youngster with a smooth swing sails two balls into the water, his second attempt ricocheting off boulders ringing the green. His wife, from the red markers (85 yards), then slaps a nice shot that lands ten feet short of the flag, skips past the hole, and rolls off the back of the green into the water. The following foursome hits two into the water from the white tees (128 yards) and yet another from the drop area at the water's edge (perhaps 50 yards), a shot that lands near the pin and skips off the back.

Paradoxically, the best result is a tee shot that hits the rocks and caroms onto the green, 10 feet from the hole.

One of the players mutters something you can't hear. Suddenly, Pete Dye jumps out from behind a rock, shrieking, "*Nobody* expects. . ."

Well, you get the idea.

What distinguishes the Stadium Course from other tough layouts is that there is no breather—all eighteen holes are right out of the Torturer's Handbook. The touring pros loathed it on sight and were successful, after one year, in getting it removed as one of the courses of the Bob Hope Classic. The PGA club pros then seized the opportunity to one-up their glamorous counterparts: They voted to stage their national championship on Dye's layout every year. "It makes them feel macho," says a well-known touring pro. "It's a little like bungee-jumping without the cord."

Many golf architects consider Dye's work at PGA West as little more than a bad joke, but Tom Fazio weighs in with an unexpected opinion. "I think Pete did a *great* job at PGA West," he says. "The client wanted something that would draw attention to the resort, and Pete delivered. And he had nothing to work with at that site, only his imagination."

Fazio may be right. In 1992, the Nicklaus Resort Course and Palmer Course at PGA West each hosted 40,000 rounds at $80 per round, but the Stadium Course drew 50,000 rounds at up to $150 a round. Asked if that meant that people enjoyed his courses more than the other designers', Dye responded, "Either that or they're crazy."

There's a theory worth looking into.

> *"The pros play golf in the air, but the weekend player plays golf on the ground. That's why I'm not into perpendicular hazards. It creates more air golf."*
> —Tom Fazio, golf architect

THE TPC NETWORK: TAKING A MULLIGAN

"When you contrive a disaster, it's not as pleasing."
—*Deane Beman,*
PGA Tour Commissioner

Breakfast is hardly the time to write off an epoch. Neither is it the best hour for confession. But when Deane Beman declared that the Era of Obstacle Golf had ended, he did it over juice and toast in a hotel coffee shop in Chicago. A fastidious man, Beman even managed to eat a little crow without spotting his tie.

"I don't want to be too harsh, I don't want to minimize my respect for the architects' talents," he said, fork poised over his plate. "But I believe today that golf course architecture is overdone. And, unfortunately, we helped push architecture toward the extreme with the original Tournament Players Club. Which I regret."

By "we," Beman meant himself and the PGA Tour's Tournament Policy Board, which oversees the Tour's international network of Tournament Players Clubs. Since the original stadium course, TPC at Sawgrass, opened in Ponte Verde, Florida, in 1980, the Tour has built, bought, or licensed seventeen TPCs and has four more in development. The guiding concept behind this turfgrass land rush has been "stadium golf," a Beman-inspired concept that evokes either admiration or loathing, depending on whether one approaches the idea with a tournament ticket or a golf club in hand.

"The greatest players in the world can *play* our golf courses," Beman said, "but they don't *enjoy* playing them. The influence of Sawgrass, the heroic philosophy, has led to disaster holes at every turn. You either make a birdie, or you make a six or a seven. We think we have a responsibility to change that trend. From this day forward, our philosophy—when we have complete control—will be to build traditional golf courses."

That sound you hear, the crumbling noise, is the Berlin Wall falling, George Bush saying, "*Don't* read my lips," and the Loch Ness monster caught sunning on the beach at Waikiki. Beman is the man who once called the TPC at Sawgrass "the Yankee Stadium of golf." He's the guy who said, "The public wants to see a player fight through adversity."

The other sound you hear, the wild cheering, is from the touring pros. The players have long complained that stadium courses are unappealing to the eye, gimmicky, and poor tests of golf. Any TPC glossary includes the noun "moonscape," the adjectives "stark," "severe," and "artificial," and the pejorative compounds "cookie-cutter holes" and "island greens." Tom Watson once said he would like to take a bulldozer to the greens at Sawgrass. Greg Norman thought dynamite would improve the ninth hole of the TPC at Avenel in Bethesda, Maryland. Scott Hoch, asked if he thought a certain TPC suited his game, answered, "I don't know what it suits, other than a goat."

Since many players earned their Tour cards on stadium courses (the Tour's annual qualifying school has been held on TPCs several times since 1982), you might expect the pros to show some fondness for the layouts. But no.

"We're choosing guys for the Tour from these courses," says Paul Azinger, a reluctant veteran of three Q-schools. "A lot of good players aren't making it because the luck factor is involved too much. Guys you would expect to make it, don't."

As a rule, the guardians of stadium golf have ridiculed the players' gripes. "God couldn't build a golf course that all those guys would like," says Ben Brundred, the general chairman of the Kemper Open, held at Avenel since 1987.

"You'd think they were playing a junkyard the way they holler," says PGA Tour official Mark Russell. "I ask a guy, 'Why don't you like the course?' He says, 'I made a ten there.' Is that the course's fault? Sounds to me like he hit a couple of bad shots."

Beman, the author of many eloquent defenses of stadium golf over the years, now sides with the critics . . . sort of.

"Obstacle golf and stadium golf are not synonymous," he says. "There is complete compatibility between stadium golf and traditional courses. It's just a question of taking some of the sharpness out of the design, introducing subtleness."

If Beman sounds like the dentist in the old joke— "Your teeth are fine, but your gums will have to come out"—it's because he knows stadium golf is not going to go away. It's too successful.

To understand the paradox, one must know the history. The TPC concept dates to an idea Beman had in the early sixties, which he now calls "completely unsuc-cessful." At the time, he was an insurance broker and the country's top amateur golfer. He suggested that the United States Golf Association build a series of courses around the country. The new courses would serve two functions: as sites for the U.S. Open and as "laborato-ries" for the USGA's Green Section research. That idea went nowhere, but Beman filed the thought. He also made note of another U.S. Open phenomenon of the fifties: cardboard periscopes, sold by the hundreds to fans who couldn't see the action on traditional Open courses.

In the mid-sixties, Beman took a brief fling at golf course design, in partnership with the late Ed Ault, a prolific designer of courses in Maryland and Virginia. None of the courses they planned together were built, but the two men played around with features designed solely to benefit the golf spectator.

"That's where the term 'stadium golf' came from," says Beman. "Ed wanted to put several golf holes in a vir-tual stadium. He even had roadways—people movers, almost—to move galleries around. He and I didn't see eye to eye on that. I thought it was too much of a depar-ture."

In 1967, at age 29, Beman wandered off to play pro-fessional golf for six years. (He won four PGA tourna-ments.) He emerged in the seventies as Commissioner of the Tour, a post he has held for more than twenty years.

Beman and his staff plotted a strategy for the Tour's growth based upon television exposure and corporate sponsorship of tournaments. But they saw a problem: The courses on which many Tour events were staged were too small. Corporate hospitality required two or more acres for tents. Sponsors paid top dollar for distant spectator parking sites. Television called for production pads, crane positions, and routing for miles of cables. Tournament administration needed headquarters space and dispatching areas for a thousand-plus volunteers. Concessions required a staging area and numerous on-course sales sites.

The average course of 120 to 160 acres barely had room for the spear carriers, much less daily galleries of 30,000 or more. Small galleries, Beman knew, meant smaller purses. So did rising "use fees," the Tour's euphemism for rent. (Sponsors currently pay as much as $250,000 for a course—unless it's a TPC, which is rent-free.)

Beman's response was to resurrect his old "laboratory course" idea. In 1978, the Tournament Policy Board authorized the construction of a golf course next to the Tour's headquarters in Ponte Verde Beach. The new course, in addition to housing the Tour's own Players Championship, would be a testing ground for various concepts, which have since been packaged as stadium golf: spectator mounds, amphitheater greens, spectator amenities.

The architect of choice? Pete Dye.

"I hired Pete because of Harbour Town," Beman says. "The consensus of the players was that Harbour Town [on Hilton Head Island, South Carolina] was the best new course and Pete Dye was the A-number-one best architect."

Working with the flat, featureless swampland of northeastern Florida, Dye cut down trees, dug up tons of sand, filled the holes with water, and piled the debris alongside the fairways for spectator mounds. That was fine, but for greens he put in coffee tables. For greenside bunkers, he installed underground missile silos.

"Frankly, when Pete got in there, he didn't build a Harbour Town," says Beman. "I spent half my time toning down what he was imagining. I don't know what was in Pete's mind. The product we opened was *very* severe, particularly the greens. But it was toned down a lot from what it would have been if I hadn't been alarmed."

Dye chuckles at this account. "I assure you," he says, "when we built the greens at Sawgrass, Deane and everybody looked at them and approved them. I didn't go out and build eighteen greens and they caught me. And when I built the island green, nobody disapproved. Maybe I should have said, 'This is very severe,' but I thought we were all in accord. Anyway, there wasn't a green at the TPC as severe as the seventeenth green at Medinah. And we were thinking about Bermuda grass at that time, which would have been slower. It was built when there was still a nebulous hope that courses wouldn't go toward faster and faster greens."

If Beman was alarmed, the touring pros were traumatized. Ben Crenshaw called it *Star Wars* golf and said the course was designed by Darth Vader. Jack Nicklaus said, "I've never been very good at stopping a five-iron on the hood of a car."

The greens at Sawgrass have since been softened, but elements of Dye's demonic design have crept into subsequent TPC courses: heroic water carries, steeply banked greens, severe putting surfaces. Where once a deft chip would suffice, architects now ask players to fly the ball high from tight lies onto shelflike greens. "There was no such thing as a sixty-degree wedge on Tour until these courses came along," says Azinger. "Golf was not meant to be played on different tiers like that."

The unanticipated result of Dye's work at Sawgrass was that it started a trend toward super-difficult golf courses. Beman faults *all* the architects for that, not just Dye. "They kept trying to outdo each other. The extreme became the norm as they tried to one-up each other. That's the battle we've been fighting all along."

If any one hole engages the two sides of the controversy, it is Dye's seventeenth at the TPC at Sawgrass— the notorious island-green par 3. This is the hole where Robert Gamez shot an eleven. This is the water hole amateurs replenish with tears.

But is the seventeenth any less fair than the par-3 sixteenth at Cypress Point, which calls for a heroic carry of 205 yards from one cliff edge to another, often in gale-force winds?

Yes, says Beman, because the hole at Cypress Point enjoys the authority of natural terrain. The hole at Sawgrass does not. It is the product of men with bulldozers. "When you *contrive* a disaster, it's not as pleasing," he says. Beman might have added that Alister Mackenzie provided the sixteenth at Cypress with a small fairway at the left front of the green for bailing out in conditions of extreme hardship. The seventeenth at the TPC at Sawgrass offers no such sanctuary.

The debate goes on, but it is hard to argue with the commercial success of the TPC network. The golf courses took in almost $43 million in 1989, $6.3 million of which was profit. More important, the stadium courses have fulfilled their promise as handlers of large galleries. The TPC in Scottsdale, Arizona, sold 109,000 tickets for the Saturday round alone of the 1990 Phoenix Open. That's about as many spectators as attend all four rounds of an average U.S. Open.

But more is not always better, and savvy golf fans are getting wise to the trade-offs inherent in stadium golf. Yes, more people can crowd around an amphitheater green, but the gallery ropes must be set much farther back to preserve the sight lines for the mound folk. On a stadium course, you'll never see a spectator with a periscope, but you'll see dozens with binoculars. Want to sit in the shade? At most TPC courses, you can forget it. Trees block the views from the spectator mounds.

In fact, if the 1990 U.S. Open had been played on a stadium course instead of old-fashioned Medinah, Hale Irwin could not have slapped palms with thrilled galleryites after sinking his long putt on the seventy-second hole. He would have had to cut short his celebratory jog or risk falling into a moat.

The lack of intimacy is easily explained. Traditional courses have their greens on high ground to encourage drainage. Stadium courses have their greens on low ground to provide visibility. "That leads to drainage problems," says Irwin, who has his own golf-course design company. "You have to put a catch basin below the green to carry off rainwater. That's why you end up with a steeply banked green that usually repels golf shots."

And because spectators can't see much from the grassy ditch around the green, they have to watch from some far-off hill.

AMERICA'S WORST GOLF COURSES

Another shortcoming: When tournament week ends at Medinah or St. Andrews, workmen come and tear down the grandstands; the terraced berms and ugly mounds are permanently there on stadium courses, hogging the view and looking abandoned.

Nowhere were these defect more obvious than at the TPC at Avenel in Potomac, Maryland. Designed by Ed Ault Associates with Beman himself as an uncredited consultant, Avenel endured unrelenting criticism in its first four years. Although tournament attendance soared when the Kemper abandoned nearby Congressional, the Tour's marquee names voted "no" with their feet. The typical field included only three or four of the top twenty money winners, despite the Kemper's million-dollar purse and network television. Avenel has since been remodeled.

Other TPCs have fared better. Scottsdale's, designed by Jay Morrish and Tom Weiskopf, looks almost natural in its desert setting. Bob Cupp's StarrPass in Tucson— which is no longer a TPC— has that desert-terrarium look that Jack Nicklaus popularized at Desert Highlands in Scottsdale. Memphis's Southwind, designed by Ron Prichard, has been well received.

Ironically, when asked to name his favorite TPC, Beman doesn't hesitate: "The first one, Sawgrass." Most of the tournament players agree, even those who loathed the course in its original form. "I love that course," says Azinger. "It's now one of my favorite courses, when it's in shape."

Beman hopes that the Tour, by stressing "traditional values" from the start, can avoid extensive redesign work at future TPCs. The existing TPCs are being redone gradually, in consultation with former tournament win-

J O H N   G A R R I T Y

ners, until a more subtle design is achieved and the language of the golfers becomes less blue.

Necessarily, the new golf courses will take longer to be appreciated—which, Beman says, may not sit well with either the golfers or the developers. "They want instant recognition, but impatience doesn't create great golf courses. It took Donald Ross thirty years to perfect Pinehurst Number 2. People think he went out there one day with a few mules and built this great course, but he *lived* there and kept working at it."

Golfers at Thornapple Creek Golf Club in Kalamazoo, Michigan, can be forgiven for watching the maintenance crew carefully during overseeding. The original four owners and the club pro were convicted a few years back for "intent to distribute two hundred thousand pounds of marijuana." The course, seized by the federal government, was sold to a management firm in 1988, but is still called "Club Fed" by many.

The twelfth hole at Kansas City's Royal Meadows used to be a 240-yard par 3 into the prevailing wind with a fence-line OB to the right and a ditch in front of the green. "And the greens out there are postage stamps pushed up by a farmer who didn't use any dirt," says a knowledgeable source, "so they're almost vertically sided."

A new tee was constructed, and the hole now plays at an undistinguished 180 yards.

AN INTERVIEW WITH JOHN DEMATTEO

Before he played Pied Piper and drove the rats off the Dyker Beach Golf Course (and into the Bay Ridge section of Brooklyn), agronomist John DeMatteo got a look at the other end of the golf business, the more sublime. "I used to work at Pinehurst," he says, "and I got real interested in Donald Ross courses. There's one in Detroit, Rackham Park, that I got to work on when I went out there to give American Golf a hand. There's some great history in these old courses, and I love to study the similarity of designs." Today, DeMatteo lives near Golf House, in New Jersey, and practices agronomy for the Loft's Seed Company.

Q: Having worked at Pinehurst, was it jarring to take on New York City's municipal courses?

A: I was from the New York area, I was used to it. The California people, *they* had the culture shock. They hated it.

Q: What was your job with American Golf?

A: I was what they call the regional superintendent. I was in charge of organizing all the maintenance on all the courses and all the grounds. I hired the superintendents, helped coordinate between the city and American Golf, negotiated things.

JOHN GARRITY

Q: *You took over some golf courses that looked like war zones. Any horror stories?*

A: I can't remember exactly what the first horror was. The first crazy incident happened the day after we got there, at a golf course on Staten Island. Somebody torched some garbage cans that were sitting right next to the maintenance building, and the maintenance building—well, you'd have to see it. It's an old, old barn that was already gutted out and lousy looking. No heat or anything. They torched the garbage cans, the barn caught fire, and the new course manager called the fire department, who came and put it out. I kidded the guy, "You shouldn't have called, you should have sat and watched it burn! Thrown some chairs on it or something!" It's the biggest mistake he ever made.

Snowmobile tracks at LaTourette Golf Course, Staten Island, New York. (Copyright John DeMatteo)

AMERICA'S WORST GOLF COURSES

Q: What's the story with the rats?

A: There's a golf course called Dyker Beach in the Bay Ridge section of Brooklyn, right at the base of the Verrazano Bridge. If you know where to look, you can see it from the bridge. It's certainly not a poor area of Brooklyn, there are lots of nice homes. Anyway, there's a road that goes all the way around the golf course, a road where people jog. The weeds had grown up, and people used the roadside as a dump. They'd park their cars there on a Saturday, change the oil, and just leave the stuff. There were batteries and oil cans, concrete, bricks—anything they didn't want to pay to haul away.

We were responsible for everything inside the fence line at all the golf courses, so we had mowed all the grass and made everything nice and neat. Then some councilman or somebody jogged around the place and insisted that the roadside be cleaned up. We got into a bunch of legal baloney over that, because the city said, "We're not going to do it, it's your problem." So I had to bring in crews from all the other golf courses for this project. We had to walk through and pick up all this debris before we could even take a mower in because it would have wrecked the machinery. We spent two solid weeks hauling that stuff away. Next thing you know, the city is getting all kinds of phone calls from people complaining that rats are coming into their homes, and they want us to stop cleaning the roadside so the rats will go back. Meanwhile, I'm out on the golf course in the mornings, driving along the fence line, and the rats are hopping around like bunnies.

Q: What did you do?

J O H N   G A R R I T Y

A: We cleaned the whole place. I don't know where the rats ended up.

Q: *Once you got the courses cleaned up, what did you have?*

A: Most of them turned out to be really nice golf courses. There's architectural work on them that could never be duplicated today. Really neat things, like the mounding on some of the greens. Nobody goes in and handworks mounds any more, it's all machinery, and that limits you in certain ways. The greens at Pelham, I think, are the most interesting. Split Rock has some great stone work, these amazing aqueducts that carry water under Route 95 and across the courses. Nobody but the parks people knew it was even there.

Q: *What about the course designs?*

A: Fantastic. The only course I thought was lacking in the layout was Clearview, in Queens. That course used to be a lot bigger, but they had to eliminate some holes when they cut in the Clearview Expressway. But it's still a beautiful public course, about 5,200 yards. They put about 95,000 people around it every year, and everybody is happy.

Q: *Years of poor maintenance must have obliterated the design subtleties.*

A: That's true. When we took over the golf courses, a lot of the bunkers had filled in with grass. They never cleaned them out and they never raked them. And then

AMERICA'S WORST GOLF COURSES

we found all these little mounds around the bunkers. What we finally figured out was that someone had gone and edged them one time and then dropped all the clippings in one spot. But they never bothered to pick the clippings up. Two weeks later, they just mowed over them, and so you had all these little mounds. That's the kind of thing that happened.

Q: *You've worked in other parts of the country. Where are the worst courses found?*

A: Florida and Texas probably have some of the ugliest golf courses that you ever want to see. All they've done to

The Number 1 tee, on the roof of the clubhouse at the East Course, Grenelefe Golf and Tennis Resort, Grenelefe, Florida.
(Copyright Bill Amick)

J O H N   G A R R I T Y

develop a golf course is plow up the ground and plant some Bermuda grass. And you can grow that on almost anything.

They don't want any maintenance or help. They're just mowing grass and trying to get greens fees.

Q: *You've probably seen some pretty bad golf holes in your time.*

A: Quite a few, from a design standpoint. There's a course on the eastern shore of Maryland, Harbourtowne Resort, that's like a Pete Dye course before he ever did golf courses. That has some unusual holes. If I remember correctly, there's a double-dogleg par 4. You have to hit a knuckleball off the tee, sort of hook it and slice it with one shot. I tried to hit a 4-iron there, but I hit it though the fairway and had to kick out and hit it again. Whoever heard of a double dogleg on a par 4?

Another hole that doesn't make sense to me is one that Rees Jones did at Jones Creek, outside Augusta. It's a par 4. You hit off the tee and it's straight down a hill. You get down to the bottom, and you have to go straight up again. It's one of those holes he probably had to put in and didn't really like.

A hole that was really bad was this par 3 they built at the TPC at Southwind, in Memphis. I rode around the course with [PGA Tour Commissioner] Deane Beman and Bobby Weed, who was in charge of construction. We pulled up at this par 3, and it was just terrible. The rest of the course was nice, but this par 3 was straight and boring. It had a stupid mound in front of it, and the green was flat and completely without character. You looked at it and wondered, "Where did this come from?" The Memphis Classic was coming up, and Beman just sat there staring at this ridiculous hole. Finally, he said, "The last day of the tournament, I want the dozers sitting behind that green."

Q: Getting back to New York, how do you rate those courses now—ten years after your salvage job?

A: I think they're pretty good now, as good as they were two years after we took over. Maybe they've even improved because of some of the programs I started. They've straightened them out, gotten all the graft and corruption out of the system, and gotten them to where people can go out and have a decent round of golf. But it's virtually impossible, financially, to put them back in

Sand bunker with intrusive vegetation on Number 13, Clearview Golf Course, Queens, New York, circa 1985. (Copyright John DeMatteo)

J O H N   G A R R I T Y

super shape. The city doesn't want to spend any money on them, and American Golf is not going to spend a lot on structural improvements.

It's a shame, because these are golf courses that people should see.

> "Waterfalls. . .are created nowadays in areas with neither water nor a place for it to fall. One Ted Robinson layout in Palm Springs even has more waterfalls than holes."
> —Tom Doak, Golf magazine contributing editor

THE JAPAN EIGHTEEN, GAME BOY CLUB

Par 72, 6,453 yards

Unusual features: No caddies, no carts, no starter, no half-way house, no driving range; but practice is allowed on the course

Greens fees: None. Unlimited golf with $25 initiation fee

Curious fact: No ball has ever been hit off the property

"Did Pete Dye design this course?"

That's just one of the imprecations muttered by frustrated golfers after a round at the world-renowned Japan Eighteen. Indeed, both of the courses at the Game Boy Club—the resort-style Japan Eighteen and the tougher American Eighteen—resemble a Dye layout, despite the absence of railroad ties. Hard, steeply sloped greens seem to repel shots, even when struck with pronounced backspin. Water comes into play on almost every hole, and trees choke off the most logical routes of attack.

"I wouldn't even call it golf," complained one Missourian after a recent round. "On one hole, I drove into the right rough, leaving a carry of two hundred-sixteen yards over a lake to a heavily bunkered green. I then hit four straight three woods—each one as good as I can hit it, just *nailed*—and all four landed in the water. I wound up making twenty-two on the hole."

A golf writer for a well-known sports magazine stalked off the course after making 7 from the first cut of rough on number 4. "I hit the perfect drive!" he sputtered. "Dead center, a slight draw, and it rolled into this stuff, this so-called rough, that must be a product of

American Wire. I tried to hack my way out with a nine-iron, and the ball went forty yards."

Complaints about the Nintendo-grass rough have been commonplace since the Japan Eighteen opened in 1991. "I've tried every club in the bag," says one middle-handicap player, "and you just can't hit the ball more than a hundred yards out of it." Others moan about the tight landing areas, changeable winds, and the inane background music that plays incessantly over the club's PA system.

The course plays longer than its 6,453 yards. The 468-yard second, a par 4, generally requires *two* shots

Hole Number 3, The Japan Course, Game Boy Club.
(John Garrity, Copyright 1993)

with the driver, even for a long hitter. "And you wouldn't believe the number of holes that call for a long-iron off the tee and a wood for the approach shot," says a frustrated regular. "I wouldn't play this course again, *ever*— except the course next door is even worse."

The only aspect of play at the Japan Eighteen that gets good marks is the putting. Despite the humped-up appearance of the greens, the ball rolls true and 3-putts are a rarity. "I can't remember the last time I missed one inside six feet," says one notorious yipster. "I just step up and knock 'em in."

Oddly enough, given the Japan Eighteen's reputation for difficulty, numerous sub-par rounds have been recorded, most of them by junior golfers. The course record is sixty-two, shot by a fourteen-year old from Osaka, Japan. "And that was in the usual swirling winds," says a club spokesman.

Even Desmond Muirhead hasn't built a course this weird. Yet.

PONKAPOAG GOLF CLUB
Canton, Massachusetts
36 holes, par 71, 6,400 yards; par 72, 6,600 yards
Rounds per year: 120,000 over two eighteens
Grass type: Suicidal rye overseeded with bent (and battered) grass

Ponkapoag Golf Club, sportswriter Rick Reilly points out, is only twenty minutes from The Country Club at Brookline, venerable site of major golf championships. But there are differences.

"At The Country Club, for instance, you drive up to the clubhouse, where the boy meets you and takes your bag. At Ponky, you give a boy your bag only at gunpoint."

Ta-da-*boom*.

"At Ponky," Reilly continues, "the greens look like barber school haircuts."

Chick-chicka-*boom*.

"At Ponky—"

But no, it's not fair. As a provider of rim-shot rhetoric, Ponkapoag (pronounced PONK-a-pog) is right up there with Rodney Dangerfield's wife. Golfers who have never set foot on its thirty-six sparsely grassed holes know about Ponky's sandless sandtraps, its hopeless drainage, and those 150-yard markers "that aren't one hundred-fifty yards from anything in particular." They know because they read Reilly's 1988 *Sports Illustrated* article, "The Missing Links," which used Ponkapoag to paint a picture of daily fee golf in America.

Funny story. But reading between the laughs, one got the sense that Ponkapoag was a victim of malice and neglect on a Dickensian scale. Operated by the Metropolitan District

Commission (MDC), a tributary of the Commonwealth of Massachusetts, Ponky seemed to suffer fools at every level— indifferent managers, incompetent greenskeepers, indolent counter personnel. Golf jobs were handed out as patronage plums, causing one player to characterize Ponky as "a summer drop-off spot for every politician's son, brother-in-law, cousin, and niece." The long-suffering golfers, despairing of relief, helped out with maintenance, even going so far as to buy flagsticks and rakes. Their reward: a place in the 3 A.M. line that formed for morning tee times.

Conditions have improved, we are pleased to report—thanks largely to the *SI* story, which forced embarrassed officials to take corrective action. But Ponky lovers tend to dwell on past hurts.

"Nobody *cared*," says Jack Neville, head pro at Ponkapoag since 1979. "Light bulbs were missing, there was no heat in the clubhouse, the grass wasn't being mowed—and nobody in authority cared." So bad was the situation when Reilly visited that Neville asked not to be quoted in the story. "There was nothing positive I could say about this place," the pro says with a shrug.

J O H N   G A R R I T Y

Neville's view is shared by outsiders. "For years it was a place where they just hid people on the MDC payroll," says *Boston Herald* sportswriter Joe Gordon. "They had one guy, who was there for a lifetime, who basically pushed a wheelbarrow. Other workers only came by to pick up their checks." As a result, Ponkapoag's championship eighteen—a classic Donald Ross design with a stretch of strong finishing holes—took on the look of a derelict. "One year, Ponky was in line to get the U.S. Public Links Championship," Gordon recalls, "but the USGA took one look at the place and said, 'Forget it.' "

Enter state senator Bill Keating, who pushed a bill through the legislature that hiked greens fees—a move made palatable by an order that all revenues thus raised be put back into the golf courses. ("A revolutionary concept," says a cynical observer of Massachusetts politics.) Under the direction of an energetic new recreation director and a hard-working club manager, the patronage employees have been driven off and hundreds of thousands of dollars spent on improvements. Even a catastrophe—a clubhouse fire, a few years back—has

at Mission Hills is the permanent site of the LPGA's Dinah Shore Championship; and Nicklaus commands the highest fee of any course designer in the world: $1.25 million per job.

Even their harshest critics acknowledge that all three are professionally competent and capable of inspired work. Dye and Nicklaus courses tend to be well-constructed, pleasing to the eye, and challenging—too challenging by half, some would say. Both men are blamed for building "monuments to their egos"; both men are considered "punitive" designers; and both are regarded as trial-and-error builders who frequently have to re-do their own courses. ("I spend ninety percent of my time going back and fixing my mistakes," Dye admits.) Both men are expensive; Nicklaus is still trying to live down his reputation, earned early in his design career, as led to meaningful rehabilitation. "We've got central air, rugs, and everything!" marvels Neville, the loyal pro.

What Ponkapoag still lacks is *grass*—that essential ingredient for a good golfing experience. "When Mother Nature is the sole determinant of its condition, Ponky is in pretty good shape," says the *Herald*'s Gordon. "In other words, April, when melting snow and spring showers keep it green." He sighs heavily. "But it always deteriorates by June."

Fellow sports scribe George Kimball is even blunter in his condemnation: "It's awful. It's desperate."

The problem, of course, is that Ponky's turf has long been tended by the golf-industry equivalent of hospital candystripers—well-meaning but unskilled laborers. Neville says his constant lobbying for an experienced course superintendent used to make his superiors frown and ask, "What do you mean by a course superintendent?" Neville's reply: "A person with a degree in agronomy who knows how to grow and maintain grass."

Miraculously, Ponkapoag hired just such a person in 1993, stirring hope among golfers that the days of dusty tees, bumpy fairways, and rock-hard

J O H N   G A R R I T Y

greens will soon pass into memory. But as this book went to press, sad old Ponky was still in intensive care. Says Kimball, "As long as a hundred thousand people a year tramp through that place, it's going to be a tough salvage job."

No joke.

> During his 1990 campaign, Massachusetts gubernatorial candidate William Weld demanded that state prison officials stop "coddling" inmates with lavish amenities like cable television and gymnasiums. At the top of Weld's hit list was the "three-hole golf course" at Norfolk State Prison, a layout that campaign rhetoric elevated to resort status.
>
> Subsequent to Weld's election, officials plowed up the Norfolk course. Or rather, they rolled it up. "It wasn't really a golf course, as such," says Department of Corrections spokeswoman Robin Bavaro. "It was a practice strip like you'd have in your backyard. It had a few holes in it where they practiced putting."
>
> The Norfolk course record, shared by several inmates, is 3.

The shortest par 4 in the world, according to Golf *magazine, is the 210-yard tenth hole at Hillandale Golf Club, Greenville, South Carolina. "The fairway turns 90 degrees left 170 yards from the tee, and the dogleg is guarded by trees, forcing players to hit a mid-iron followed by a wedge into the green.*

"Poor golfers love difficult golf courses," says difficult golf course architect Pete Dye. "That's something the touring professionals don't understand. The eighteen or nineteen handicapper can't break par, so what he's looking for is the shot. He holes out of a trap somewhere, and he forgets about the other ninety-three shots. He made par at the Calamity, and that's the shot he goes home with."

The curious, tepee-shaped fairway mounds at the Loxahatchee Club, a Jack Nicklaus design, inspired one Tour player to say the seventh hole looked "like a meeting of the Indian nations." Cruder minds have described Loxahatchee as "a walk down mammary lane."

JOHN GARRITY

Z-BOAZ GOLF COURSE
Fort Worth, Texas

Par 70, 6,033 yards
Dominant aromas: Fried fish and furniture varnish

"Riding on its reputation."

That's what you hear whenever Z-Boaz shows up on the latest list of America's worst courses. And it's true—this vintage layout has suffered numerous improvements since its debut as a WPA project in 1937. The spindly trees have grown into impressive oaks; ponds and creeks have filled with water; once-faceless sand bunkers now yawn impressively. It's a far cry from the hardpan heaven that earned Z-Boaz the nickname "Goat Hills New."

Richard Teague, the muni's current assistant pro, looks out the clubhouse window and shakes his head

Warning sign, Z-Boaz Golf Course, Forth Worth, Texas.
(John Garrity, Copyright 1993)

AMERICA'S WORST GOLF COURSES

over the changes. "When I played here, there wasn't no trees," he says. "Wasn't no grass either, for that matter."

What Z-Boaz has going for it is its legacy. In a memorable article in *Sports Illustrated* called "The Glory Game at Goat Hills," writer Dan Jenkins recalled his student days at nearby Texas Christian University, where he and his band of rowdy, bet-happy ne'er-do-wells wasted their afternoons on the parched fairways of the old Worth Hills Golf Course.

Overtaken by development—not to mention good taste—Worth Hills went under the bulldozers some years ago, causing *SI* to remark that "it was nice to learn that *something* could take a divot out of those hard fairways." Z-Boaz carries on the tradition as best it can. Every summer, Jenkins invites a touring pro and a bunch of lesser lights to Z-Boaz for a one-day tournament, the Dan Jenkins Partnership & Goat Hills Glory Game Reprise. Although not as bleak as Worth Hills in its prime, Z-Boaz still offers a pungent contrast to Fort Worth's elegant Colonial Country Club, some miles away. No clipped hedges and high-dollar homes here— just a stark rectangle of Texas hill country bounded by a railroad line and three busy streets.

The din of traffic, in fact, is an inescapable feature of golf at Z-Boaz. The neighborhood is rich with furniture showcases and warehouses, most of which provide a pleasing backdrop to the golfer about to play a shot. Batting cages, miniature golf, and a life-size statue of a giraffe enhance the northern boundary, while empty storefronts and a karate school line the seventh fairway on the east side. And where, save for the finishing holes at Cypress Point, will the golfer find two more natural

Sixteenth green at
Z-Boaz Golf Course.
(John Garrity, Copyright
1993)

Seventeenth green at Z-Boaz Golf Course. (John Garrity, Copyright 1993)

greensites than Z-Boaz's sixteenth (at the foot of the neon "Checks Cashed" sign) and seventeenth (hard against Long John Silver's Seafood Shop)?

Surely, this is what Robert Louis Stevenson meant when he described Z-Boaz as "the most beautiful meeting of land and transmission shops that nature has produced."

THE LAKESIDE COURSE, BLACKHAWK COUNTRY CLUB
Danville, California

Par 72, 6,845 yards
Course rating: 74.2
Local rule: Free drop if earth moves during swing

One of the truisms of golf course design is that money usually buys results. So Lakeside *should* be in the *Golf Digest* Top 100. Everything about the Blackhawk development screams opulence: two golf courses, two clubhouses, two tennis complexes, two swimming pools, and a mansion behind every eucalyptus tree. Football commentator John Madden lived here (until he sued the developer over cracks that kept appearing in the walls of his house). Other recent residents include Oakland A's reliever Dennis Eckersley, San Francisco Warriors star Chris Mullin, and, before the divorce (and the trade), baseball slugger José Canseco.

Pricey? As recently as 1989, members had to cough up $40,000 to join Blackhawk—more than most of the courses in this book would fetch at auction. If he wanted to, the Lakeside course superintendent could top dress the greens with shredded hundred dollar bills.

So Blackhawk's 950 members must grit their teeth when visitors complain about bumpy greens, blind shots, unreachable par 3s, and bunkers filled with water. Senior tour player Bob Wynn dismisses Lakeside with a single word: "Disneyland." Lesser players have employed stronger words. "It's not the worst course in the world," says *Valley Times* sports editor Ted Johnson, "but it's probably the most disappointing."

The Lakeside Course seemed jinxed from the start. Built in 1981 from a plan by respected designers Bruce Devlin and Robert Van Hagge, the hilly layout immediately began to sag like a bad facelift. Earth slides on the third and thirteenth holes interrupted construction. The twelfth tee melted in a rainstorm and washed down to the green. Fairway bunkers, halfway up the fifth hole, slid 300 yards back to the tee.

And talk about a tough-driving course. Former major leaguers Dwayne Murphy and Mike Heath once rolled a golf cart at Lakeside. "A million dollars worth of ballplayers upside down in the mud," recalls a Bay Area baseball writer. "How's that for publicity?"

Not surprisingly, there has been a lot of finger pointing. "They built the houses first and then built the course to fit," says *San Francisco Examiner* columnist Art Spander. "And it didn't fit."

"The Lakeside opened too early," concedes Blackhawk board president Frank Straface. "But that's typical of a housing-driven course—you want to get on it first to sell houses."

These days, golfers want to get *off* Lakeside first and onto Blackhawk's other course, the Falls, a pleasing Ted Robinson layout. Those who get stuck at Lakeside have to contend with five par 3s, four of which are 215 yards or longer. "There's one par three, over water, that I can't reach with a full driver," says Spander. And if that sounds like a hacker's gripe, consider the testimony of golf legend Lee Trevino, who played Lakeside in a charity Pro-Am. The organizers had parked five red BMWs by the first tee—prizes for holes-in-one made on any of the par 3s. Trevino walked by after his round, glared at the cars, and snapped, "They should give me a couple of fucking hubcaps just for hitting the greens!"

The most maddening of the par 3s is probably number 12, which calls for a downhill shot of 180 yards to a small green balanced atop a ridge. Shots that miss the putting surface roll 60 or 70 feet down either side. From these valleys it's difficult to hold the green with a chip, so players routinely play back and forth across the green, like bored children throwing a ball over a house. "It's fun to watch from the tee," says Johnson. "But when *you* do it, you wind up biting a sand wedge."

The sixteenth is almost as memorable—a 220-yard par 3 with a green that can't be seen from the tee. Long hitters have to respect the out-of-bounds behind this hole. "There's nothing quite like launching one right over the flag," says one grudge bearer, "and watching it sail out of bounds."

But the hole that best characterizes the Lakeside course is the fifteenth, a narrow, uphill par 5 of 620 stupefying yards. A 3-wood third shot is commonplace here, and shots that fall short land in a dry creek. Standing on the fifteenth tee, a few yards from a $3.6 million Tudor mansion, the player can't help speculating on the role that golf plays in the lives of the wealthy. "It's really a piece of work," says Johnson.

Blackhawk is still plagued by slides. As of January, 1993, the initiation fee had slipped to $30,000.

JOHN GARRITY

If you've enjoyed *America's Worst Golf Courses* and would like to nominate your own special course for consideration for Volume 2 of this book, please mail us your course description and all the details. Write to:

> America's Worst Golf Courses
> c/o Macmillan/Collier Publishing Co.
> 866 Third Avenue
> 21st Floor, Mail Stop #4
> New York, NY 10022

INDEX

J O H N   G A R R I T Y